FLYING FOXES

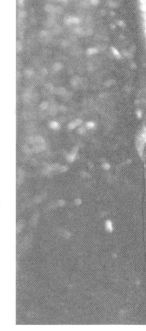

AUSTRALIAN NATURAL HISTORY SERIES
Series Editor: Professor Terence J. Dawson

The function of this series of titles is to make accessible accurate scientific information, complemented by high quality illustrations, on a wide variety of Australian animals. Written and illustrated by trained researchers and scientists, the series is intended for students and biologists at both secondary and tertiary levels and, in general, for readers with a serious interest in animals and the environment. Interested authors should contact the UNSW Press or Professor Dawson, School of Biological Science, University of New South Wales, Sydney, NSW 2052.

Books published in the series:

The Dingo in Australia and Asia, Laurie Corbett

Echidnas of Australia and New Guinea, Mike Augee & Brett Gooden
    Illustrated by Anne Musser

Goannas: The Biology of Varanid Lizards (2nd edition), Dennis King & Brian Green
    Illustrated by Frank Knight, Keith Newgrain & Jo Eberhard

Kangaroos: Biology of the Largest Marsupials, Terence J. Dawson
    Illustrated by Anne Musser and Jillian Hallam

The Koala: Natural History, Conservation and Management, Roger Martin & Kathrine Handasyde
    Illustrated by Sue Simpson

Little Penguin: Fairy Penguins in Australia, Colin Stahel & Rosemary Gales
    Illustrated by Jane Burrell

The Mountain Pygmy-possum of the Australian Alps, Ian Mansergh & Linda Broome
    Illustrated by Katrina Sandiford

The Platypus: A Unique Mammal (2nd edition), Tom Grant
    Illustrated by Dominic Fanning

Pythons of Australia: A Natural History Geordie Torr
    Illustrated by Eleanor Torr

Sea Snakes, Harold Heatwole

The Wombat: Common Wombats in Australia, Barbara Triggs
    Illustrated by Ross Goldingay

FLYING FOXES

FRUIT AND BLOSSOM BATS
OF AUSTRALIA

Leslie Hall and Greg Richards

Illustrated by Louise Saunders

UNSW
PRESS

This book is dedicated to the late Harry Frith and John Calaby, who supported our enthusiasm for bats, and allowed us the time and resources to establish our interest in flying foxes; and to Dr Ken Myers, who tolerated our distractions and absences from his rabbit research team in our early days at the Division of Wildlife Research, CSIRO, Canberra.

A UNSW Press book

Published by
University of New South Wales Press Ltd
UNSW SYDNEY NSW 2032
AUSTRALIA
www.unswpress.com.au

© Leslie S. Hall and Gregory Richards 2000
First published 2000

National Library of Australia
Cataloguing-in-Publication entry:

Hall, Leslie S.
Flying foxes: fruit and blossom bats of Australia.

Bibliography.
Includes index.
ISBN 0 86840 561 2.

1. Flying foxes—Australia—Identification. 2 Bats—Australia—Identification. I. Richards, Gregory. 1949–. II. Title. III. Fruit bats and blossom bats of Australia. (Series: Australian natural history series).

599.40994

Printer Everbest Hong Kong

CONTENTS

ACKNOWLEDGMENTS

Over the years we have had many fruitful discussions with colleagues regarding our and their research and interest in flying foxes, fruit and blossom bats. These people include MT Abdullah, J Barrett, A Borsboom, M Calford, L Collins, P Conder, G Crowley, J Donovan, H Field, R Geisel, J and R Gough, M Graydon, S Hamilton, K Haplin, N Irwin, A Johnson, L Little, H Luckhof, D Lunney, J McLean, L Martin, M McCoy, J Nelson, G O'Brien, C Palmer, J Pettigrew, P Prociv, H Spencer, K Stager and members of the Kur-ring-gai bat committee. We thank them for their friendship, information and advice. Many thanks also to Theo Allofs, Patrina Birt, Pamela Conder, Noel Chopping, Clancy Hall and Jack Pettigrew for allowing us to use their excellent photographs.

Helpful comments on the text of this book were made by M Augee, P Birt, T Dawson, P Eby, S Hand, B Law, N Markus and K Parry-Jones. We thank them for their time and comments. We have frequently used the results of their research in this book, but we take full responsibility for the final text.

ORDER	SUB ORDER	FAMILY	GENUS

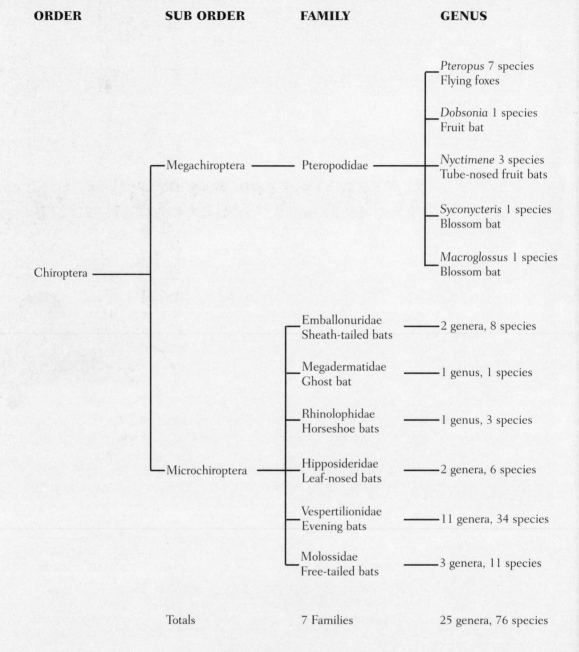

Pteropus 7 species
Flying foxes

Dobsonia 1 species
Fruit bat

Megachiroptera — Pteropodidae — *Nyctimene* 3 species
Tube-nosed fruit bats

Syconycteris 1 species
Blossom bat

Macroglossus 1 species
Blossom bat

Chiroptera

Emballonuridae — 2 genera, 8 species
Sheath-tailed bats

Megadermatidae — 1 genus, 1 species
Ghost bat

Rhinolophidae — 1 genus, 3 species
Horseshoe bats

Microchiroptera — Hipposideridae — 2 genera, 6 species
Leaf-nosed bats

Vespertilionidae — 11 genera, 34 species
Evening bats

Molossidae — 3 genera, 11 species
Free-tailed bats

Totals   7 Families   25 genera, 76 species

Figure 1.1
The cladogram shows the structure and relationships within the Order Chiroptera in Australia.
Note that there is only one family in the Megachiroptera. The number of genera and species mostly
follows Churchill (1998).

CHAPTER 1

INTRODUCTION

Bats are the only mammals capable of active and sustained flight. They do so with semi-transparent wings, composed of two layers of almost hairless skin stretched between the elongated forelimb bones, the hind limb, and the tail. The other external features of bats are not unlike those seen in many groups of other small mammals. Due to their capacity for flight, their nocturnal lifestyle, and other physiological and ecological adaptations, bats have become a very successful group of mammals. Bats make up the second most numerous mammal group in the world, after that of rodents (which include rats, mice and guinea pigs).

Bats belong to the Order Chiroptera (meaning 'hand-winged'). There are roughly 925 different species (types), divided into two Suborders: the Megachiroptera, made up of 42 genera containing 166 species; and Microchiroptera, 135 genera containing 759 species (see Figure 1.1). All of the families of both Suborders of bats found in Australia occur in other parts of the world, although some of the genera in the Microchiroptera are restricted to Australia.

Broadly speaking, microchiropterans are small, feed mainly on insects, and navigate using echolocation (animal sonar). The smallest bats in the world belong to the Microchiroptera. The bumble-bee bat from Thailand, which weighs only 1.5 grams, is possibly the world's smallest mammal. In Australia the Suborder Microchiroptera is represented by six families, 20 genera and approximately 63 species. They vary in size from the large ghost bat, weighing 120 grams, to the small forest bats, some of which weigh only 3 grams.

In the Microchiroptera, there are some species which eat plant products, and could therefore be called 'fruit bats'. These are members of the Family Phyllostomatidae, and are only found in Central and South America. This group of bats has diversified into a wide range of food habits and includes blood-feeding vampire bats, fish-eating bats, carnivorous and insectivorous bats, as well as the group of fruit eaters.

Megachiropterans are larger bats, are all 'phytophagous' (that is, they feed on plant products), and navigate principally by sight. The Suborder Megachiroptera contains just one family: the Pteropodidae. There are five genera, containing 13 species, of Pteropodidae in Australia. These are the flying foxes, fruit bats and blossom bats, and it is these that are the subject of this book.

TABLE 1.1
SPECIES OF MEGACHIROPTERANS RECORDED IN AUSTRALIA

Flying foxes

Pteropus poliocephalus	Grey-headed flying fox
P. scapulatus	Little red flying fox
P. alecto	Black flying fox
P. conspicillatus	Spectacled flying fox
P. macrotis epularius	Large-eared flying fox
P. brunneus	Dusky flying fox
P. banakrisi	Torresian flying fox
Dobsonia magna	Bare-backed flying fox

Tube-nosed fruit-bats

Nyctimene robinsoni	Eastern tube-nosed fruit bat
N. sp.	Torresian tube-nosed fruit bat
N. sp.	Cape York tube-nosed fruit bat

Blossom bats

Syconycteris australis	Queensland blossom bat
Macroglossus minimus	Northern blossom bat

Most flying foxes belong to the genus *Pteropus*. There are 65 species of *Pteropus* worldwide, many of which are restricted to islands or island groups. These have the largest body-size of all bats, and besides Australia are found on islands of the Indian Ocean as well as India, Pakistan, Nepal, Burma, South-East Asia, Philippines,

Indonesia, New Guinea, and the islands of the western Pacific Ocean (see Figure 1.2). Also included in the Australian flying foxes is a representative of the genus *Dobsonia*, which is a large bat found on Cape York.

There is a number of other large fruit-eating Megachiroptera, which are not in the genus *Pteropus* but which are also called 'flying foxes'. These bats are found in Africa, India, Pakistan, South-East Asia, Indonesia, New Guinea and some Western Pacific islands. These belong to the genera *Pteralopex*, *Acerodon* and *Eidolon*.

The largest flying fox in the world is aptly named *P. giganteus*, which is found in Pakistan, India and Burma. Males weigh 1300–1600 grams and have a wingspan of 1.7 metres. In Australia, adults of several species of flying fox can reach a body weight of slightly over 1000 grams, but their wingspans seldom exceed 1.5 metres. There are also other large fruit-bats found in Africa, but they do not reach the size of flying foxes, and they belong to different genera within the Megachiroptera.

As well as flying foxes, the Megachiroptera contains two other groups of bats, both found in Australia. These are the tube-nosed fruit bats, and two species of blossom bats. These bats are smaller than flying foxes. Tube-nosed fruit bats are very distinctive, having elevated tubular nostrils and spots of yellow on their wings, ears and nose. They have prominent bulging eyes and can weigh up to 50 grams. Blossom

Figure 1.2
World distribution of the Megachiroptera (broken line) includes Africa, the Middle East, Southern Asia, Australia and many islands. The easternmost point in the Pacific Ocean is the Cook Islands. The distribution of the flying-fox genus *Pteropus* (hatched) is more restricted. Note the absence of *Pteropus* on the African continent.

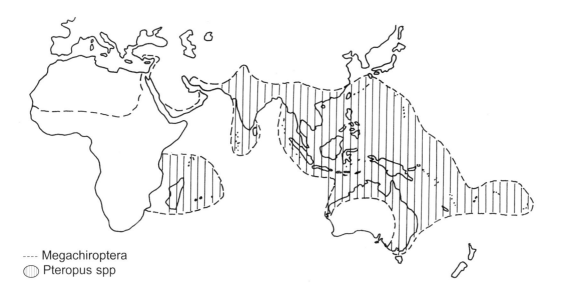

---- Megachiroptera
�illⅡ Pteropus spp

bats are some of the smallest members of the Megachiroptera. They are mouse-sized miniature flying foxes, with large forward-looking eyes and long pointy snouts. Blossom bats have uniform light brown fur and weigh up to 20 grams.

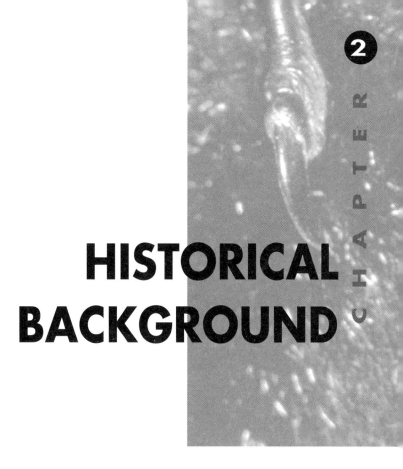

HISTORICAL BACKGROUND

EVOLUTIONARY AND FOSSIL HISTORY

The fossil record of bats is intriguing. They seem to have suddenly appeared around 58 million years ago in the earliest Eocene period (58–35 million years ago) of Europe. It can be reasonably argued that the selective pressures which favoured flight operated quickly, and this was responsible for the lack of 'in between' examples of animals with only partial wings. No fossils unambiguously linking bats to other mammal groups have been found. Possible relatives include tree-shrews (Order Scandentia), flying lemurs or colugos (Order Dermoptera), primates, and extinct groups such as nyctatheriids. The lack of fossils of early bats can also be attributed to their delicate bones, and the fact that their roosting sites would not favour the preservation of bones.

Some of the earliest fossil material identified as coming from a bat are teeth from Pakistan. The oldest fully articulated bat skeletons are those of North America's *Icaronycteris index*, which has a number of features resembling modern day megachiropterans. The fossil *Icaronycteris* had an elongated thumb, and a claw on the second digit. However, because of its basic wing structure, long tail, and shape of its molar teeth it was classified as a microchiropteran. One of the oldest fossil bats in the world was found at Murgon, Queensland by Sue Hand and her colleagues. It too is a primitive microchiropteran, thought to be more than 55 million years old and closely related to archaic Eocene bats in France and the United States.

The oldest putative fossil megachiropteran (identified by a single premolar tooth) is from Thailand, dated to the late Eocene. The next oldest is *Archaeopteropus transiens*, represented by an articulated skeleton from the early Oligocene (35–25 million years ago) of Italy. The original specimen was destroyed in World War I, but casts of it survive. There have since been finds of megachiropterans in Europe and Africa from the Miocene and Pliocene (23–6 and 5–3 million years ago), and many Pleistocene (2 million to 500,000 years ago) fossils from Africa and Asia. Pleistocene fossils from New Guinea include some from the still-living species *Dobsonia moluccensis* and *Aproteles bulmerae*.

Bats were originally thought to have colonised Australian during the Pleistocene when it was connected to New Guinea, and ocean barriers with Asia were shorter than they are today. The Murgon fossil microchiropteran puts their entry as far back as the earliest Eocene. Despite an intensive amount of searching in the masses of bat and other animal material extracted from the Riversleigh deposits (3–25 million years old) in north-western Queensland by Sue Hand and her colleagues, no megachiropterans have yet been unearthed, and as yet no extinct megachiropterans are known from Australia. Because of this, most researchers consider that megachiropterans may not have entered Australia until only recently in the late Quaternary. However, all researchers agree with the theory that the primary source of megachiropterans for Australia was undoubtedly from the north via New Guinea.

These archaic bats are usually all grouped into the Superfamily Paleochiropterygoidea. It is not clear which, if any, of these early bats gave rise to the more familiar, modern kinds of bats, including flying foxes, fruit bats and blossom bats. The older fossil history of microchiropterans is paradoxical, as megachiropterans are classically regarded as the most primitive of the two Suborders, and therefore should have appeared first in the fossil record. Most morphological and molecular data suggest that megachiropterans and microchiropterans are sistergroups (that is, they are each other's closest relatives) and that megachiropterans probably diverged from other bat lineages very early in the group's history.

However, recent research on megachiropterans (principally on flying foxes) by Professor Jack Pettigrew at the University of Queensland, has shown that the difference between megachiropterans and microchiropterans may reflect different origins for the two groups. He and his colleagues have shown that there are many differences between the two Suborders (as would be expected), but that the different features in the megachiropterans are frequently shared with primates (for instance primates and megachiropterans are born with fur and open eyes, while microchiropterans are born naked with closed eyes). There are many such similarities, particularly in the brain and soft tissues of megachiropterans and primates, which are not preserved in fossil material and have not previously been considered in their classifications. This has led to the theory that megachiropterans have evolved from a primate ancestor, and that microchiropterans have come from a different shrew-like animal, which shares more of their features (for instance some shrews are capable of producing ultrasonic calls). As yet, DNA studies do not fully agree with the primate origin of megachiropterans, but the theory has certainly been the stimulus for much research around the world.

ABORIGINAL REPRESENTATIONS

The first records of flying foxes in Australia are those found in Aboriginal rock art and mythology. In the sandstone cave galleries in northern Queensland and the Northern Territory there are numerous depictions of flying foxes, usually in groups, which reflects a natural view of the animal. However Aboriginal rock art depictions cannot be interpreted in a simple European way as representing a food source, or a message of the presence of flying foxes nearby. Although these factors are often involved, it is more likely that the representation of flying foxes in Aboriginal rock art has a deeper spiritual meaning, relating flying foxes to the environment and Aboriginal Dreaming. Archaeological studies suggest that Aborigines have been in Australia for at least 60,000 years, possibly longer. The rock art which includes flying foxes is not that old, and dates from recent times to tens of thousands of years old in well preserved art sites. Most Aboriginal communities within the range of megachiropteran distribution have stories about flying foxes. Some of them explain why these animals have wings and fly, why they only fly at night, and why they

Figure 2.1

Flying foxes are frequently depicted in Aboriginal rock art. These drawings from a cave wall on Cape York accurately show that flying foxes do not have a tail.
(Les Hall)

only feed on plant products. Often the stories are quite complex and link flying foxes with totems and spiritual icons of the Aborigines.

Archaeological excavations in northern Australia usually reveal that flying foxes were only occasionally utilised as a food source. In recent times however, there appears to be more reliance on them, with large numbers being regularly harvested in parts of the Northern Territory. This is possibly a result of the reduction of other food sources and changed hunting methods.

EUROPEAN DISCOVERY AND CLASSIFICATION

Flying foxes (genus *Pteropus*) were first described by Brisson in 1762 from specimens collected from the Reunion Islands and taken back to Europe. Many observations of flying foxes by Europeans during the early colonisation and exploration periods of Australia were probably misidentified as 'nocturnal birds'. In 1770 Captain James Cook, in one of the first records for flying foxes for Australian, described them as 'black winged powder kegs'. These were black flying foxes on the Endeavour River, North Queensland. A camp site is still there today.

The history of the scientific discovery of flying foxes in Australia reflects the country's European colonisation. In order of their discovery, the grey-headed flying fox (*P. poliocephalus*) was described by Temminck in 1825 from four specimens collected in 'New Holland'. In 1850, Gould described the spectacled flying fox (*P. conspicillatus*) from a specimen collected on Fitzroy Island. The little red flying fox (*P. scapulatus*) was described by Peters in 1862 from a specimen collected on Cape York. The black flying fox (*P. alecto*) was first described in 1837 from a specimen from Menado, Indonesia. In 1867, Peters described a black flying fox from Rockhampton as *P. gouldii*, and it was subsequently renamed *P. alecto gouldii*. The dusky flying fox was collected on Percy Island off the central Queensland coast in 1874 and described by Dobson in 1878. It has never been collected or seen since that date. Recently, the large-eared flying fox (*P. macrotis*) was found to roost on islands in Torres Strait. This bat was first described by Peters in 1867. The most recent discovery of a new flying fox in Australia was on Moa Island in Torres Strait in 1990. This species, the Torresian flying fox (*P. banakrisi*), is about to be formally described.

The bare-backed flying fox (*Dobsonia moluccense*) was described by Quoy and Gaimard in 1830 from a specimen collected on the Indonesian island of Ambon in the Moluccan Islands of Indonesia. It was first recorded from Australia in 1935. Recently it was realised that all specimens of *D. moluccense* were restricted to the Moluccan

Islands, and that specimens from New Guinea and Australia identified as *D. moluccense* were actually *D. magna*, which was described by Thomas in 1905 from a specimen collected on the Mambare River, Papua New Guinea.

The generic name for the tube-nosed fruit bats, *Nyctimene* (from Greek for 'night moon'), was assigned to this genera by Borkhausen in 1797. They are a complex group which has radiated from New Guinea and is currently regarded as having some of the oldest features of the megachiropterans. Due to the uncertainty of the identity of two tube-nosed fruit bats collected only recently in Australia, one at Rocky River on Cape York and the other on Moa Island in the Torres Strait, the history of discovery of tube-nosed fruit bats in Australia is still unfolding.

The first tube-nosed fruit-bat recorded in Australia was *N. albiventer*, a species which was originally described as *Cynopterus albiventer* by Gray in 1862. Australian specimens were later named *N. robinsoni* by Thomas in 1904, after the naturalist Robinson who collected two specimens from Cooktown. Specimens from Australia were also referred to at some time as *N. tryoni*. It was thought this species was restricted in Australia to Queensland, and was given the common name 'Queensland tube-nosed fruit bat'. It has since been found in New South Wales, and another two species of fruit bat are known from Queensland, so *N. robinsoni* is now called the eastern tube-nosed fruit bat.

It is thought that the species recently found on Moa Island could be *N. cephalotes*, which has had a long and varied taxonomic career and at some stage has also been included with *N. vizcaccia*, which was described by Thomas in 1914. The specimen from Rocky River is distinct from both *N. robinsoni* and *N. cephalotes*, but as yet has not been properly identified. Both '*albiventer*' and '*tryoni*' may be available for the two new species of tube-nosed fruit bats found on Cape York.

The Queensland blossom bat, *Syconycteris australis*, was originally described as *Macroglossus minimus* var. *australis* by Peters in 1867, from a specimen from Rockhampton. Matschie erected the genus *Syconycteris* in 1899.

The first Australian representative of *Macroglossus* was the northern blossom bat collected from Murray Island in Torres Strait and called *M. australis* by Ogilby in 1892. The Australian forms, which were also once referred to as *M. lagochilus*, have now been placed in *M. minimus*, which was originally collected from Java and described by Geoffroy in 1810.

IDENTIFICATION AND DISTRIBUTION

FLYING FOXES

Flying foxes are large bats which form very visible and noisy daytime camps where they hang totally exposed. These camps can be located in mangroves, swamps, rainforest and tall mixed forest, usually with a dense vine understorey, and often beside a creek or water. Recently camps have appeared in urban locations. (Weight and forearm length measurements given in the species accounts below are average adult male and female. Note that outside of the breeding season, males are noticeably heavier than females.)

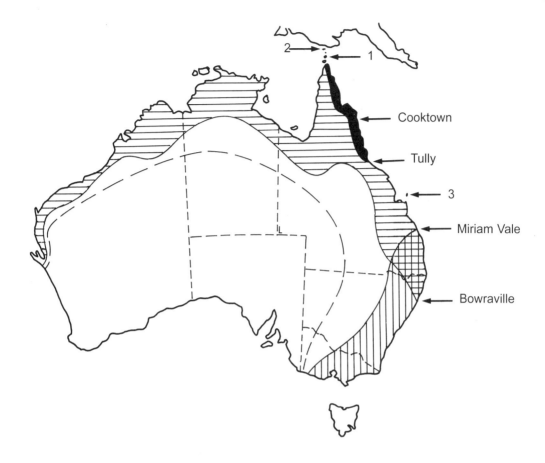

2 ← → 1

Cooktown

Tully

3

Miriam Vale

Bowraville

Figure 3.1
Distribution of
flying-fox species
in Australia.

KEY

Grey-headed flying fox

Black flying fox

Spectacled flying fox and bare-backed flying fox (north of Cooktown)

- - ‒ Little red flying fox (inner limit)

1   Torresian flying fox (Moa Is.)

2   Large-eared flying fox (Boigu Is.)

3   Dusky flying fox (Percy Is.)

BLACK FLYING FOX *PTEROPUS ALECTO*

Description
The fur of the black flying fox is generally jet black (Plate 1), but some variation does occur. A dark chocolate brown patch of fur is often seen on the back of the neck and shoulders, and brownish fur is not uncommon around the eyes and on the face. Some black flying foxes get a frosting of greyish tips all over their body fur, particularly on the belly.

Distribution
Black flying foxes are found around the northern coast of Australia, and inland approximately covering where permanent water is found in rivers. Their south-eastern limit has been moving southwards for at least the last 60 years: in 1930 the southern limit was at Rockhampton, Queensland; in 1960 it was the Tweed River in far north-eastern New South Wales; and currently it is found as far south as Bowraville, near Nambucca Heads. (See Figure 3.1.)

Weight: 500–1000 g
Forearm: 150–190 mm

LITTLE RED FLYING FOX *PTEROPUS SCAPULATUS*

Description
The little red flying fox varies from a reddish brown to light brown, and there are distinct patches of light, creamy, brown fur where the leading edge of the propatagium (wing membrane) and the shoulder meet (see Plate 2a). The head is covered with greyish fur, and in some forms found in northern Queensland, this grey fur continues down the back, giving the flying fox a frosted appearance. A distinct feature of the little red flying fox is the semi-transparent brown wings, visible when it flies during the day.

Camps
It is the only species of Australian flying fox that regularly roosts in tight clusters. At times up to 30 individuals have been seen hanging together in a tight bunch.

Distribution
Little reds are the most widespread species of Megachiroptera in Australia. In the dry inland areas, little reds are attracted to the flowering of eucalypts and melaleucas along watercourses following good rains. In more coastal areas they are also nomadic, but can be seasonal as they follow the more regular flowering of coastal eucalypts. It is dependant on the presence of good flowering of eucalypts and melaleucas, but its south-western and south-eastern distributional

limit varies extensively from year to year — it was found in north-eastern South Australia in 1968, and again in 1986. (See Figure 3.1.)

Weight: 300–600 g
Forearm: 125–155 mm

GREY-HEADED FLYING FOX *PTEROPUS POLIOCEPHALUS*

Description
This is the only species of Australian flying fox that has a collar of orange/brown fur which fully encircles the head (see Plate 2b and 3a–c). It is also the only species which has fur right down the legs to the toes. As the name suggests, the head is covered with grey fur. The belly fur is grey, often with flecks of white or ginger. The fur on the back shows two forms (which could be related to age, moult, or a subpopulation): one form has dark grey fur on the back; the other has a pronounced silver or frosted appearance.

Distribution
Grey-headed flying foxes are found in coastal south-eastern Australia from Victoria to Miriam Vale in Queensland, and inland to the western slopes. (See Figure 3.1, page 11.)

Weight: 600–1000 g
Forearm: 140–175 mm

SPECTACLED FLYING FOX *PTEROPUS CONSPICILLATUS*

Description
The spectacled flying fox is easy to identify due to the distinctive straw-coloured fur which surrounds the eyes (see Plate 4). The species can also have varying amounts of the same pale fur on the shoulders and the head. It is not uncommon for the eye rings of some individuals to be indistinct, making them look similar to black flying foxes.

Distribution
In the wet tropics north of Tully, camps of the spectacled flying fox are always found in or close to rainforest and sometimes in mangroves associated with black flying foxes. There are records of individuals and small camps of spectacled flying foxes as far west as Chillagoe, where they were associated with black flying foxes. (See Figure 3.1, page 11.)

Weight: 500–1000 g
Forearm: 155–180 mm

LARGE-EARED FLYING FOX *PTEROPUS MACROTIS*

Description

This is a small flying fox which has brownish fur all over the body (Plate 5). The head can appear slightly darker because of greyish fur. The ears are large (31–37 mm).

Distribution

Following recent surveys in the Torres Strait area, a camp of the large-eared flying fox was located on a mangrove island beside Boigu Island. This is their only known site in Australia. (See Figure 3.1, page 11.)

Weight: 315–415 g
Forearm: 136–142 mm

DUSKY FLYING FOX *PTEROPUS BRUNNEUS*

Description

The fur is mid-brown, slightly lighter on the belly, with a reddish-gold tinge due to pale tips on the hair. There is a slightly lighter mantle of brown fur, which partly conceals buff-coloured glandular tufts of fur at the sides of the neck in males. The upper side of the leg is furred for three-quarters of its length.

Distribution

The dusky flying fox was only ever seen in 1874 on Percy Island, off the Queensland coast between Rockhampton and Mackay, and the above description comes from a specimen, which may have faded, that was collected at that time. There were reports in the late nineteenth century that it was still common on the island, but no further specimens were ever collected. Its probable extinction is unfortunately a familiar pattern in the genus worldwide, emphasising the tenuous nature of flying-fox survival on islands. (See Figure 3.1, page 11.)

Weight: probably about 200–300 g
Forearm: 118 mm

TORRESIAN FLYING FOX *PTEROPUS BANAKRISI*

Description

This is a small, black coloured flying fox (Plate 6) with relatively long ears (28 mm) and a long thumb (48 mm). The base of the fur is dark brown, and the fur on the belly often has grey tips or frosting.

Distribution

This is a newly discovered flying fox, found on Moa Island in Torres

Strait in 1990, which is to date its only known range. (See Figure 3.1, page 11.)

Weight: 210–240 g
Forearm: 128–141 mm

BARE-BACKED FLYING FOX *DOBSONIA MAGNA*

In Australia, the bare-backed flying fox, is still frequently referred to as *D. moluccense*. It is a large bat which is difficult to distinguish from flying foxes in the genus *Pteropus* at night. It feeds on flowering euca-lypts and fruiting trees, and makes loud flapping sounds when manoeuvring around food trees.

Description

These flying foxes are dark brown to almost black in colour, with very dog-like facial features (Plate 7). The wing membranes meet in the midline of the back, giving it a hairless covering of its back. These fly-ing foxes have only a single pair of upper and lower incisors. They have a short tail. The claws on the feet, thumb and first digit have a distinct pale colouration.

Camps

Most records of roost sites for this flying fox are from large boulder piles or cracks in rocks, often covered in vegetation. There are also records of bare-backed flying foxes roosting in an abandoned mine near Coen.

Distribution

The bare-backed flying fox is found north of Cooktown (Black Mountain) to Cape York, with a doubtful sighting recorded further south and inland at Chillagoe. It frequents well timbered areas and rainforest containing boulder piles, rocky overhangs and cracks in remote areas on the east coast of Cape York. The species is also found in New Guinea where it is regularly hunted in caves for food. (See Figure 3.1, page 11.)

Weight: 350–500 g
Forearm: 135–155 mm

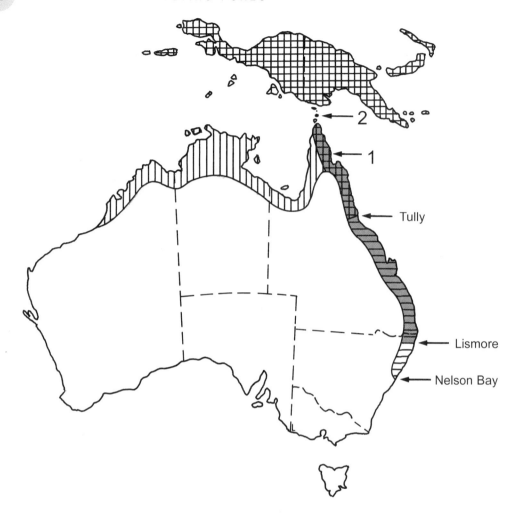

KEY

■ Eastern tube-nosed fruit bat

▤ Queensland blossom bat

▥ Northern blossom bat

1 Cape York tube-nosed fruit bat (Silver Plains)

2 Torresian tube-nosed fruit bat (Moa Is.)

Figure 3.2
Distribution of
tube-nosed fruit bats
and blossom bats in
Australia
and New Guinea.

TUBE-NOSED FRUIT BATS

Tube-nosed fruit bats are easily recognised by their unusually long tubular nostrils. Another feature is the occurrence of light yellowish spots on areas of bare skin, such as the ears, nose, and wings. No two tube-nosed fruit bats have the same pattern of spots. The fur is light brown, often with a darker stripe down the middle of the back. Skull morphology is the most accurate way to identify the species, which are otherwise difficult to separate live in the hand without comparative specimens. (Weights, and forearm and tail length measurements, are again adult male/female averages.)

EASTERN TUBE-NOSED FRUIT BAT *NYCTIMENE ROBINSONI*

Description
The fur of the eastern tube-nosed fruit bat (Plate 8) is a light brown, slightly paler on the belly, and frequently with a stripe of darker fur down the midline of the back. The wings have a brown background with a variety of coloured spots and blotches, varying from yellow to dark brown. There are distinct light yellow patches on the ears and on the tubular nostrils. A small tail protrudes from the fur between the hind legs.

Distribution
The eastern tube-nosed fruit bat is found from the remnant Richmond River sub-tropical rainforests in far north-eastern New South Wales, up the Queensland coast to Cape York. It is more abundant in the northern part of its range, particularly in the wet tropics. (See Figure 3.2.)

Weight: 30–50 g
Forearm: 60–70 mm
Tail: 20–25 mm

TORRESIAN TUBE-NOSED FRUIT BAT *NYCTIMENE SP.*

Description
This fruit bat (Plate 9) is quite distinctive from *N. robinsoni* with which it is sympatric on Moa Island, Torres Strait. Its fur is a light fawn colour, as opposed to light brown in *N. robinsoni*. Although this species has a darker stripe of fur on the lower back, this is not as distinct as in other tube-nosed fruit bats. Its wings and tail are similar to *N. robinsoni*.

Distribution
The distribution of this and the Cape York tube-nosed fruit bat are yet

to be fully determined. At this stage, the Torresian tube-nosed fruit bat appears to be restricted to Moa Island. (See Figure 3.2, page 16.)

Weight: 40 g
Forearm: 60–65 mm
Tail: 15–20 mm

CAPE YORK TUBE-NOSED FRUIT BAT *NYCTIMENE SP.*

This species has only been caught in the East McIlwraith Lowlands on Silver Plains Station, where it is sympatric with the eastern tube-nosed fruit bat (*N. robinsoni*). When specimens were first captured, it was the slim head that first drew attention to it being a different species. The separation of this species from *N. robinsoni* has been confirmed by mitochondrial DNA. There is little doubt that further survey work on the east coast of Cape York, and a closer inspection of specimens of *Nyctimene* from this area in collections, will reveal additional specimens of this species.

Description
Morphologically, this species is very similar to *N. robinsoni*. Their external measurements are almost identical, but the fur colour is slightly lighter than *N. robinsoni*, there are less spots on the wings and ears, and it can be distinguished by its much slimmer head and procumbent incisors.

Distribution
The Cape York tube-nosed fruit bat appears to be restricted to coastal areas near Coen, and possibly extending to the tip of Cape York. (See Figure 3.2, page 16.)

Weight: 40 g
Forearm: 60–65 mm
Tail: 15–20 mm

BLOSSOM BATS

The facial features of blossom bats resemble those of flying foxes in miniature, with large forward-looking eyes, rounded ears, and a pointed muzzle. They are small brown bats which do not appear to have a tail. The Queensland and northern blossom bats have similar external features, but their skulls and dentition are markedly different. (Forearm measurements are averaged adult male and female.)

QUEENSLAND BLOSSOM BAT *SYCONYCTERIS AUSTRALIS*

Description
The Queensland blossom bat (Plate 10) is covered with light to reddish brown fur which is slightly lighter on the belly. It has a surprisingly large set of upper incisors and reasonably large canines. There is a pronounced difference in the height of the first and second incisor teeth on the bottom jaw.

Distribution
The Queensland blossom bat is only found along the east coast, from mid-New South Wales to Cape York. (See Figure 3.2, page 16.)

Forearm: 38–43 mm

NORTHERN BLOSSOM BAT *MACROGLOSSUS MINIMUS*

Description
The northern blossom bat (Plate 11) is also covered with light to reddish brown fur with a slightly lighter belly. It has an elongated muzzle and a reduced dentition (that is, fewer and smaller teeth). This bat has small incisors which are spaced apart. It also has a small, rudimentary tail which can be felt in the fur between the legs.

Distribution
The northern blossom bat is found right around the coast of Australia north of about latitude 18° South (approximated from Tully to Broome). (See Figure 3.2, page 16.)

Forearm: 38–43 mm

NOTES ON DISTRIBUTION

Although Australia is a large continent, only a small proportion of its 7.6 million square kilometres is permanently inhabited by megachiropterans. Suitable habitat is generally found only along eastern and northern coastal regions, in sub-tropical and tropical environments. Much of this habitat is dominated by myrtaceous eucalypt forest and woodland, but rainforest is also present in scattered fragments.

The relationship between the distribution patterns of megachiropterans and these types of forests leads to the notion that strong ecological relationships exist between the two, either as mutualism or co-dependence, and that this relationship has existed for a long period of time (see 'Hypothesis of co-dependence', Chapter 8). It is possible that flying foxes colonised Australia as a result of the emergence of eucalypts as a dominant plant species. Current research on nectar production and pollination mechanisms indicate that the lifestyle of flying foxes and eucalypts are closely linked.

EXTRALIMITAL DISTRIBUTION

Of the seven flying-fox species found in Australia, four are known from areas outside the country. The little red, spectacled, large-eared, and black flying foxes have all been found in New Guinea. Black flying foxes are also found on the Indonesian islands of Sulawesi, Bawean, Kangean, Lombok, Sumba and Savu, but these are considered a different sub-species. The spectacled flying fox is found on the Indonesian Moluccan Islands, north-west of New Guinea. There have been records of little red flying foxes in New Zealand, undoubtedly blown over the Tasman Sea from eastern New South Wales. The bare-backed flying fox is also widespread in New Guinea, and a number of offshore islands.

Until they are fully described, it will not be known if the two new tube-nosed fruit bats collected on Moa Island and at Silver Plains will be found extralimitally. It is likely that they could be represented in New Guinea where there are similar difficulties in tube-nosed fruit bat identification.

Both the Queensland and northern blossom bats are widespread in New Guinea and offshore islands such as New Britain and New Ireland, and the Indonesian island of Seram. However, the northern blossom bat's range extends further, throughout the Indonesian and Philippine islands and onto the south-east Asian mainland in Malaysia, Thailand and Vietnam.

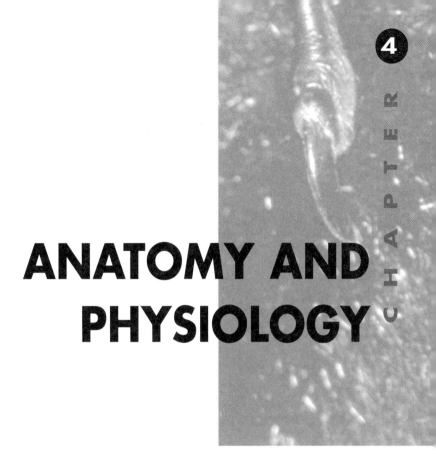

CHAPTER 4

ANATOMY AND PHYSIOLOGY

ANATOMY OF FLIGHT

Four groups of animals have taken to flying as a means of locomotion: insects, the extinct *Pterosaurus*, birds, and bats. Each group has developed a different type of wing. Insect wings are membranous sheets of chitin braced by intricate patterns of chitinous veins. Pterosaurs, which are now regarded as having been more a soaring and gliding reptile, had a membrane supported along the leading edge by a modified forearm with an extended fourth finger. Strength and support of the Pterosaur flight membrane was given by parallel strands of a keratin-like fibre. Bird wings are formed by feathers supported by a simplified forelimb skeleton along the leading edge, while bat wings are sheets of skin braced by the five-digit forelimb (Figure 4.1, page 22).

The wings of megachiropterans contain all the elements of the mammalian forelimb and have been highly modified for flight. The bones of the wing, with the exception of the thumb, are elongate and slender. All the bones of the wing are exceedingly thin and most are hollow (Figure 4.2, page 23). The main bone of the forearm is the radius. The ulna is a fine bone which is fused to the radius over most

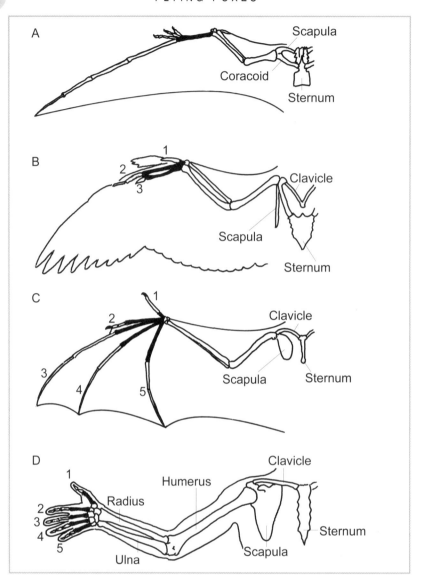

Figure 4.1
The forelimbs of the extinct Pterosaur (A), a bird (B) and a bat (C) showing how the forearm of each has been modified for flight, and a human (D). Metacarpal bones are shown in black and digits are numbered for comparison. Note that the fourth digit supports the wing of the Pterosaur; in the bird it is mainly the second; and in the bat it is all four digits.

of its length. At the elbow is a special bone found in bats called the ulnar sesamoid. This small bone, along with some small ligaments, prevents the wing from being over-extended at the elbow. The prominent thumb is larger in megachiropterans than in microchiropterans. The thumb controls the shape of the propatagium. The thumb has two phalanges and a large curved claw, but all the other digits have three phalanges. There is also a small claw on the second finger — and this is a characteristic feature of nearly all megachiropterans. The long fingers are widely spread during flight and closely folded during rest, requiring a great flexibility of the carpus or wrist.

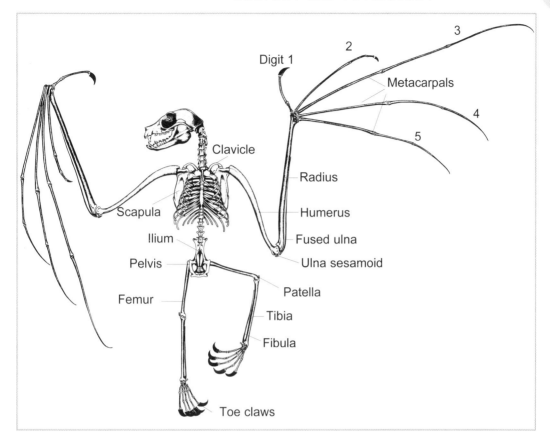

Figure 4.2
The bones of the skeleton of the black flying fox (*Pteropus alecto*) are extremely delicate. Note the absence of a tail, and the elongated finger (metacarpal) bones.

The scapula of bats is held further forward of the rib cage than in other vertebrates, and is attached to the manubrium by the clavicle. The clavicle acts as a major transmitter of the force of the wing to the body during the downstroke. The main flight muscles are attached to the sternum, as occurs in birds, but there is no keel on the sternum in bats.

The three flight membranes of Megachiroptera (Figure 4.3, page 24) extend from the body and hind limb to the arm and fifth digit (plagiopatagium); between the fingers (dactylopatagium); and from the arm to the occipitopollicalis muscle and thumb (propatagium). In Microchiroptera, the tail is connected to the legs by a fourth, broad membrane (uropatagium) which is used during abrupt changes in flight direction while pursuing insects. There is no such membrane in Megachiroptera, but it is represented by a small flap of skin down the inside of the leg. The occipitopollicalis muscle, which is responsible for keeping the leading edge of the wing taut, runs from the base of the skull, down the neck, along the leading edge of the wing and attaches to the wrist at the base of the thumb.

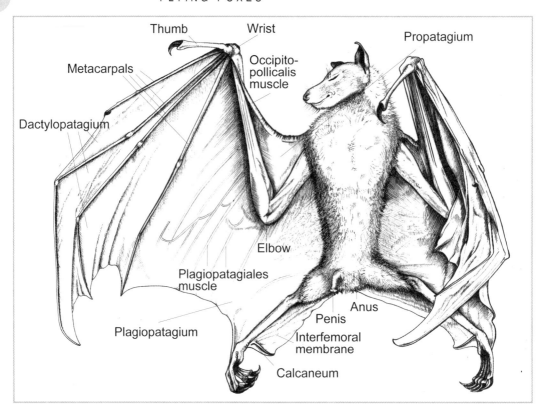

The wing membranes are composed of a double layer of almost hairless epidermis (surface skin), sandwiching a thin layer of connective tissue. The surface epidermis of the wing is quite thin, pigmented and in flying foxes at least, produces its own water-proofing agent. The connective tissue also contains blood vessels, nerves, slips of skeletal muscle (*M. plagiopatagiales*) and a criss-cross network of elastin fibres.

The patterns of these elastic fibres vary between megachiropterans, but they serve the same essential functions in all species. To be aerodynamically efficient, the wing membranes of bats must be moderately rigid when fully spread. The membrane must be strong enough to resist tearing under the stresses of flight, and from normal wear and abrasion. It must also be elastic and flexible enough to fold into a compact bundle when the bat is at rest. The ability of the wing membrane to perform these tasks is mainly due to the remarkably complex pattern of elastin fibres that reinforce all areas of the flight membrane. The muscles bracing the wing membranes are well developed and serve to anchor the network of elastic fibres. The elastin also accommodates stretching of parts of the wing when crash landings are made amongst branches.

Figure 4.3
The external anatomy of a male spectacled flying fox (*Pteropus conspicillatus*). Note the large thumb, the claw on the second digit, and the lack of a tail.

In the bare-backed flying fox the almost naked skin of the wing membranes extends to the midline of the back where the wings meet and join along the spine, resulting in the bare-backed appearance. By joining along the spine the surface area of the wings is substantially increased, and provides this flying fox with an extra amount of lift without changing the wingspan or wing shape. This extra wing area makes these bats capable of slow manoeuvrable flight which is necessary in their roost sites amongst and under large boulders. In these confined roost sites, bare-backed flying foxes are capable of hovering and flying backwards as they search for a place to hang. This slow-flying ability and manoeuvrability also allows this species to forage under the canopy in closed rainforest — a niche not accessible to other flying foxes which are quicker and less manoeuvrable. When flying around food trees, bare-backed flying foxes make a characteristic clapping noise which is caused by the wings generating lift — much the same as heard when pigeons take flight.

On both surfaces of the wings of flying foxes are hundreds of small microscopic hairs, each emerging from a lump on the skin, and which appear to be mechanoreceptors. These hairs are found principally on raised areas (such as along wing bones) and allow flying foxes to monitor air flow over the wing surface during flight. These hairs operate in much the same way as sailors use short lengths of string on their sails: by watching when the wind is blowing the string free of the sail, the sailor knows what the wind pressure is doing on the sail.

Rigidity of the outstretched wing during flight is also partly controlled by the specialised elbow and wrist joints, where movement is limited to the anterior-posterior plane. This also eliminates any need for additional musculature to rotate and brace these joints.

Although the wing-beat cycle in bats and birds is basically similar, the problem of developing effective muscular control of the wings has been solved differently in each group (Figure 4.4, page 26). The power stroke of the wings is the downstroke. In birds the downstroke is powered by the pectoralis muscle, which originates on the sternum and inserts on the humerus. In bats the muscles and their attachments are quite different. The three largest muscles of bats — the pectoralis, the subscapularis and the posterior section of serratus anterior — produce the downstroke. The first two muscles insert near the proximal end of the humerus and pull it downward. The serratus anterior however, does not attach to the humerus but originates on the ribcage and inserts on the lateral border of the scapula.

The upstroke, which is more of a recovery stroke, is largely powered by the deltoideus and trapezius groups, and the supraspinatus and infraspinatus muscles. Much less power is needed in the upstroke as the muscles are assisted by the force of the airstream. The serratus

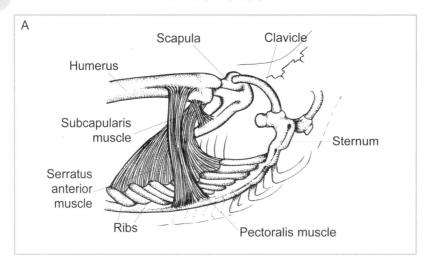

A

Scapula

Clavicle

Humerus

Subcapularis
muscle

Sternum

Serratus
anterior
muscle

Ribs

Pectoralis muscle

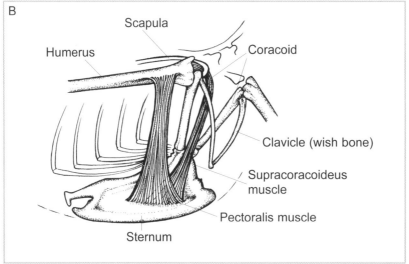

B

Scapula

Coracoid

Humerus

Clavicle (wish bone)

Supracoracoideus
muscle

Pectoralis muscle

Sternum

Figure 4.4
Muscles involved
in flight of a
black flying fox (A),
compared to those
of a crow (B).
The courses
of major flight
muscles are shown
from their origin to
point of insertion.
(The pectoralis
muscle has been
reduced to allow
other muscles and
anatomical features
to be shown.)

anterior stops the upstroke by pulling the lateral border of the scapula downwards and by doing so, initiates the next downstroke.

FLYING ABILITY AND BEHAVIOUR

Flying foxes can propel themselves at 25–30 kilometres per hour in normal conditions, and up to 40 kilometres per hour downwind in a light breeze. In a wind tunnel, grey-headed flying foxes can maintain a constant flying speed of 26 kilometres per hour for 4 hours. Gliding is only occasionally seen when a flying fox comes in to land on a roost tree, or when it dips down to drink over a large creek or river. Gliding is also seen in the early morning when flying foxes return to their roost. They glide down to their roost after approaching the camp from their cruising height.

Flying height above ground varies depending on topography, but is usually about 30–40 metres when foraging and 60–80 metres when travelling longer distances. In open areas flying foxes will fly close to the ground, as testified by the numbers found caught on barbed-wire fences. This is particularly common in little reds, which also fly low over water (see Mortality, page 48).

Flying foxes, with the exception of the bare-backed, rarely attempt tight aerial manoeuvres. Tube-nosed fruit bats and blossom bats — with their shorter broader wings — are capable of quick changes in direction during flight. The bare-backed flying fox, *Dobsonia magna*, has the ability to fly extremely slowly, to the point where it almost hovers, and this species can also propel itself backwards. This has been observed when the bat is approaching a roost site in a cave or while flying around a food tree. The effort required by this large bat to perform such manoeuvres results in quite loud flapping. To gain additional wing surface area *D. magna* has its wing membranes attached along the midline of the back, instead of along the side of the body as in other flying foxes.

OTHER USES OF WINGS

The wings of flying foxes, like all other bats, contain many blood vessels. When flying foxes are hot, they increase the flow of blood through the wing blood vessels to promote heat loss. When they need to cool their wings, and thus reduce the temperature of the blood, flying foxes fan their wings or let them droop to allow heat to dissipate.

On cold and windy days, when flying foxes want to retain body heat, they wrap their wings around their body and reduce the blood flow in their wings. When roosting, *Nyctimene* always wraps its wings completely around its body. The wings of *Nyctimene* are perhaps the most colourful of all bats, covered by spots and splotches of light and dark brown, yellow, and pale green. The mixture of the different hues of these colours seen on outstretched wings forms an extremely colourful pattern. When the wings are folded around the body, this pattern provides excellent camouflage. The pattern of colours in their wings closely resembles flecks of sunlight on and patterns in dead leaves.

The wings of flying foxes are also quite often brought into use during the birth of young. The wings are used as a cradle and help the newborn find a nipple. Following attachment to a nipple the newborn clings side-ways across the mother's chest. The mother covers the newborn with her wings which protects and keeps it warm, as the newborn has only a limited ability to maintain its own body temperature.

Wings wrapped around the body make an ideal raincoat. In rain, flying foxes usually hang by one leg only, tucking the other leg under the wings and thus making the 'top' of the raincoat leakproof.

Outstretched wings are also used for a some social behaviour. Open wings and a snarling face are obvious threat postures. When fending off unwanted intruders, such as other flying foxes or snakes, wings are flapped in the direction of the intruder.

The thumb, which is located on the wing, is also versatile. In climbing around vegetation during feeding or at the daytime roost the wings are folded and the thumb becomes the main hooking device for the arm. When urinating and defecating, flying foxes hang 'right-side-up' by their thumbs. Following a few deft shakes of the body, they then resume hanging upside-down. The thumb is sometimes used for grooming, mainly for scratching the few areas that the hind feet cannot reach.

Modifications of the mammalian forelimb into a wing make it, to a great extent, useless for its original purpose — walking. However, megachiropterans can drag themselves or scurry across the ground. The megachiropteran equivalent of the human palm can no longer be used as a support for walking, so the bats uses the front margin of their wrist. Of the fingers, only the thumb touches the ground, as the other fingers cannot bare any weight. The fingers are turned backward and folded close along the outer side of the radius. As a result the fingers (except the first and second) lose their pads and nails. Flying foxes can also swim quite well, using their wings in an oar-like manner.

FEET

Because the forelimb is highly modified, the hind limb (foot) is used as the main method of grooming in bats, although the thumb is also used. The hind limbs of megachiropterans are quite thin and lack any muscle bulk (see Figure 4.3, page 24). The five toes are laterally compressed and their claws are prominent. The hind limbs support and keep the trailing edge of the plagiopatagium taught during flight. The highly reduced, or absent, patella (knee cap) on the hind limb allows great flexibility and body-coverage during grooming. It is considered that the lack of bulk in the hind limb was an evolutionary adaptation to reduce weight and to centralise the body weight around the wings. This has resulted in the necessity of bats to hang upside-down. Also the small diameter of the femur makes it unable to tolerate compression stresses which would be imposed on it by alternate roosting positions.

The feet of flying foxes possess a locking mechanism for the claws on the toes. The leg tendons, which contract the claws to a right-angle for hanging onto a branch, pass through a tunnel of tissue which has a system of knobs that match similar protrusions on the tendons. This ratchet mechanism locks the toes and, with the added curvature of the claws, prevents the bat from slipping off its perch. (This locking mechanism is the reason why flying foxes hang for so long after they have been electrocuted on power lines.) To release their grip on a branch, flying foxes have to flap their wings and become horizontal to remove the pressure of their body weight from their legs, and thus release the locking mechanism from their claws.

CARDIOVASCULAR SYSTEM

Bats have a typical mammalian cardiovascular system. Their hearts are large, and relative to body weight are some of the largest found in mammals. The heart beat rate at 30°C is 130 per minute for a grey-headed flying fox and 170 for the little red. These rates are low compared to microchiropteran bats. The spleen is a very large and lies close to the stomach. The wings are highly vascular and the blood vessels in the wings are important in thermoregulation (as discussed above).

It was once thought that bats had a series of valves in their blood vessels which prevented blood rushing to their heads when they were hanging upside-down. No such valves have been found and it is considered that the size of bats and the small amount of blood involved allows them to hang upside-down for long periods.

Flying foxes are known as homeotherms, that is they are like humans and continuously regulate their body temperature at a constant high level. The body temperature of grey-headed and little red flying foxes is maintained between 35 and 40°C, even when exposed to temperatures as low as 0°C. The resting active body temperature of grey-headed flying foxes is around 36°C. Panting and wing-fanning commences when the body temperature goes above 38.5°C. Young grey-headed flying foxes quickly develop the ability to contend with cold weather and have the ability to shiver 15 to 17 days after birth. It is important that young stay close to their mother for body warmth prior to this stage.

The clustering behaviour of little red flying foxes while roosting is well known. They cluster in groups of up to 30 bats in both cold and hot weather. The combined weight of these dense clusters — often supported by only one or two individuals in the centre who are clinging to a branch — may result in the branch breaking. How this behaviour is used in their thermoregulation has not been evaluated.

For a long time it was thought that all megachiropterans were homeothermic (maintained a constant body temperature). However, recent studies have shown that both Australian blossom bats will enter torpor (that is drop their body temperature and general body metabolism) as a means of conserving energy. Torpor is a well known energy saving strategy used by mammals where they allow their body temperature and metabolic rate to fall to low levels during parts of the day or night when at rest. Then, using internal heat production, they warm themselves up just before their next activity period.

The Queensland blossom bat will allow its body temperature to drop to 18°C (from a normal 34.9°C), and the northern blossom bat will drop its body temperature to 22°C. Torpor in these bats was demonstrated by reducing food intake or dropping the ambient temperature to below 26°C. When testing for seasonal variations, it was found that bouts of torpor in summer are longer (an average of 7.3 hours), than those in winter (5.5 hours). It is thought that this was a result of less time being needed for feeding in summer months. Rewarming times are fast, over 1°C per minute, and indicate that blossom bats are likely to use day-time torpor on a regular basis.

The ability of lowering body temperature and metabolic rate has also been seen in the eastern tube-nosed fruit bat. Tube-nosed fruit bats will drop their body temperature both at night and during the day (even in summer months) after they have eaten and groomed themselves. This reduction of body temperature not only saves energy, but is possibly a means to escape the attention of predators and parasites which depend on body heat as a way of detecting their prey or host. Rewarming rates from a torpid state are very rapid in tube-nosed fruit bats, which would also be a good survival strategy.

SKELETON AND SKULL

Apart from those skeletal features for flight already discussed, there are a number of other interesting skeletal specialisations found in Megachiroptera.

One characteristic of the skeleton of bats is the rotation of the femur so that the hind limb flexes in the 'wrong' direction (ventrally). The patella is reduced or absent. This arrangement allows bats to face outwards when hanging upside-down, and when they are on the ground their feet have the claw uppermost. This also allows the body to be rotated while hanging without changing grip.

The pelvic girdle is very small and differs between male and female flying foxes. In females the pelvic girdle is an open V-shape, while in males it a closed O-shape. There is no tail in flying foxes, but tube-nosed fruit bats have a short thin skeletal tail (20–25 millimetres), while the northern blossom bat has a small stub of a tail hidden, but able to be felt, in the body fur.

Male flying foxes have a baculum (small disk-shaped bone) in the tip of their penis, the shape of which is characteristic to each species. The baculum changes slightly in size and shape due to age.

Figure 4.5

The skull of a female black flying fox (A) shows the large eye orbit, wide spacing of teeth, large canines, and incomplete postorbital process characteristic of megachiropterans. The more robust skull of eastern tube-nosed fruit bat (B) results from the powerful muscles attached to the jaws used for crushing fruit. The skulls of the northern (C) and Queensland (D) blossom bats have long pointed snouts compared to the blunter nose of fruit bats. Note also the small cheek teeth of the northern blossom bat.

SKULL

One of the prominent features of the flying fox skull is the large frontal orbits for the eyes (Figure 4.5). The orbit is not visibly enclosed but the postorbital process demarcates the upper posterior margin. This is a feature found in less specialised mammals such as insectivores. The auditory bulla is reduced to a small ring.

The skulls of tube-nosed fruit bats are very distinctive and reflect their fruit-eating lifestyle. The bulky musculature of the head is an indicator of the tube-nosed fruit bat's ability to deal with extremely hard fruit when necessary. The sagittal crest, which runs down the centre of the skull and where the jaw muscles attach, is very pronounced.

The skull of the northern blossom bat has a long pointed nose and a reduced number of teeth, which indicates that the bat is principally a nectar feeder.

A

BLACK FLYING FOX
(Pteropus alecto)

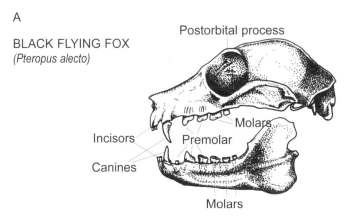

Postorbital process

Molars

Incisors   Premolar

Canines

Molars

B
EASTERN TUBE-NOSED
FRUIT BAT
(Nyctimene robinsoni)

C
NORTHERN BLOSSOM BAT
(Magroglossus minimus)

D
QUEENSLAND
BLOSSOM BAT
(Syconycteris australis)

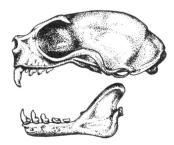
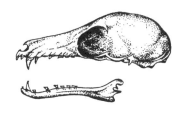
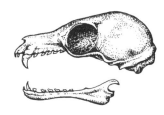

TEETH

Flying foxes have 34 teeth. These are set widely apart in the tooth row, instead of being in close contact with one another as in the Microchiroptera (see Figure 4.5, page 31). The canines are long and recurved, which is surprising for an animal which principally feeds on nectar from blossom. It does indicate however, the ability of canines to help carry fruit away from fruiting trees. Their dental formula of the upper tooth row is: incisors = 2-2, canine = 1-1, premolars = 3-3, and molars = 2-2. The lower tooth row has the same number, but with an extra molar (3-3). Abnormalities in the number of teeth are not uncommon in the little red flying fox, where both more and less teeth have been recorded. The upper first premolar in flying foxes is very small and deciduous, and is therefore often absent from the skulls of adult animals.

Unlike the oblique shear of insectivorous bats, or the antero-posterior shear of the carnivorous ghost bat, the basic flying-fox molar pattern presents an outer and inner ridge separated by a shallow, rounded longitudinal furrow (Figure 4.6). During mastication the ridge fits closely into the opposing furrow and very efficiently crushes any plant material. This is a unique mastication system among living mammals and it reflects their diet of fruit, nectar and plant products.

There are no incisors on the lower jaw of tube-nosed fruit bats, and the lower canines almost touch each other and bite against the upper incisors. Although the two blossom bats are very similar in appearance, they can be easily distinguished by the appearance of their incisor teeth. In the Queensland blossom bat the incisors are quite large and close together, while in the northern blossom bat they are spaced apart and are small (see Figure 4.5, page 31).

Annual growth rings in the dental cementum of the canine teeth of black and grey-headed flying foxes can be used to estimate the age of the animals. The process involves cutting thin sections of the tooth and counting the yearly growth rings under a special microscope. While of limited practical use for live individuals, the method does provide useful information on dead animals.

Figure 4.6

The molar teeth of megachiropterans (A: from side and above) have a smooth hollow trough with high outer and lower inner margins, or cusps. Microchiropteran molars (B) have sharply pointed cusps and usually have clearly defined W-patterned ridges.

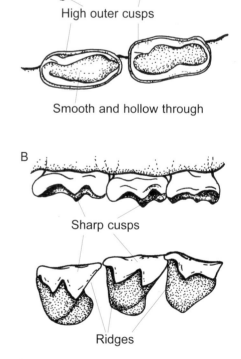

A

High outer cusps

Smooth and hollow through

B

Sharp cusps

Ridges

MILK DENTITION

Flying foxes are born with small needle-like milk teeth. These milk teeth are less complex than those found in newborn microchiropterans, in that they have no accessory cusps. All but one of the permanent premolars of flying foxes have deciduous predecessors. The milk teeth are slender and are hooked or curved at their distal ends. Their main function is to aid the young in clinging to the mother while at rest and during flight. They have no influence on the permanent teeth that replace them. Milk teeth are present at birth, commence to disappear after two weeks, and have all fallen out after four weeks. There does not appear to be any published observations of the milk dentition of tube-nosed fruit bats or blossom bats.

BRAIN, NERVOUS SYSTEM AND SENSES

The complexity of brain structures is frequently reflected in the control of the behaviour, ecology, and physiology of flying foxes, and therefore plays an important role in understanding the biology of these fascinating animals.

The shape of the megachiropteran brain (Figure 4.7) is typically mammalian, and shows some more highly developed features over that of microchiropterans. In many studies of bats, the megachiropterans have been considered rather less specialised or lower down in the evolutionary tree. The basic justification for this view is that they are less skilful fliers, in the sense that they lack the speed and nimbleness seen in many of the insect-hunting microchiropterans. However, in studies on the structure and development of the brain, it has been shown that flying foxes have the most advanced features of all the brains of Australian bats, including the microchiropterans. Very little research has been conducted at the same level on the brain of overseas bats, or other Australian groups, although current research on the brain of *Nyctimene robinsoni* indicates a number of similarities between it and that of flying foxes.

Figure 4.7
Side and top views of the brain of a black flying fox. Note the large olfactory bulb, indicating the importance of smell to megachiropterans.

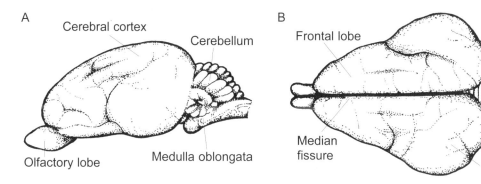

A
Cerebral cortex
Cerebellum
Olfactory lobe
Medulla oblongata

B
Frontal lobe
Median fissure
Temporal lobe

The cerebellum is a kind of computer for spatial and temporal co-ordination of posture and movements, and for muscular tone and body balance, both conscious and unconscious. Compared with terrestrial insectivores, it is well developed in all Chiroptera. This is related to the exceptionally high specialisation of bats to well co-ordinated movements in a three-dimensional space. The cerebellum is proportionally larger in megachiropterans than in microchiropterans. This is surprising given the aerial acrobatics microchiropterans perform while catching prey. However, the megachiropterans' broader spectrum of locomotion, including climbing, achieved particularly by flying foxes, seems to be of significance.

Limbic structures are areas lying deep within the temporal lobe of the cerebral cortex. Some of these structures (for instance the septum, hippocampus and schizocortex) are functionally interrelated and thought to focus on emotional states and related behavioural drives. In megachiropterans, all limbic structures are especially large and much larger than those found in microchiropterans. The relationship between the requirement of aggressive behaviour to obtain food (see The 'residents and raiders' model, page 81) and other social activities is reflected in the size of the limbic structures. Daytime roosting in trees and feeding in trees at night would seem to offer more possibility of attacks from predators or enemies, and would also require a high degree of development of a functional system engaged in a special ability for alertness.

The olfactory bulb is the primary brain centre for the olfactory (smell) system and the large size of this structure gives a good indication to the functional capacity and importance of smell in an animal. Megachiropterans have the largest olfactory lobe in the Chiroptera, but it is only proportionally equal to a terrestrial Insectivore, such as a shrew. From the large size of the olfactory lobe, it can be deduced that smell plays an important role in social behaviour and navigation, and it is the main sensory system for the location of food.

The major part of the brain is the cerebral cortex. It is concerned with the control of movement and with higher nervous functions, such as memory, pattern recognition, and vocalisation. It helps an animal interpret sensory information and perform a co-ordinated response. Much of the cerebral cortex is composed of neocortex, which is regarded as the best criterion for evaluating the evolutionary level reached by a species, as it includes the highest centres of integration. The size of the megachiropteran neocortex is by far their most advanced brain structure. The neocortex is comparatively large in megachiropterans while it is small and poorly differentiated in the insectivorous microchiropterans. The striatum and diencephalon are also especially well developed, confirming the ability of flying foxes to perform more complex neurological activities than microchiropterans.

Figure 4.8
Schematic represen-
tations of the body
surface on the
somatosensory cor-
tex of the brain of a
grey-headed flying
fox (A) and a rat
(B). These maps are
produced by stimu-
lating various parts
of the body and
recording the result-
ing nervous stimulus
directly in the brain.
The size of each
body area represents
its relative sensitivi-
ty, for instance note
the large thumb and
lip areas of A. The
location of two
somatosensory areas
(S1, S11) on the
surface of the cere-
bral cortex can be
seen in (C). (After
Calford *et al*, 1985)

The cells within the cerebral cortex of the brain that respond to information from sensors all over the body can be mapped into areas that are topologically related to the patterns formed by the sensory receptors over the body. These maps can be represented by drawing a homunculus, or a schematic representation of the body surface on the somatosensory cortex of the brain (Figure 4.8). This map is not faith-ful to the bodily proportions of the bat, as the separate areas are dis-torted in relation to the amount of sensory input from various parts of the body. The map gives a visual representation of the relative sensory importance of different areas and parts of the flying-fox body (for instance, how important the thumb is in its multiple uses in climbing, grooming, fighting and so on).

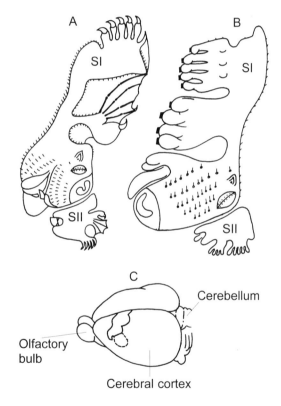

There are three separate representations of the body surface in the somatosensory map in addition to the multiple representations in the auditory (hearing) and visual areas. In all mammals the organisation can be crudely summarised by a distorted representation of the body surface with the head lateral (to the side), tail medial (to the middle), and the digits of the hands and feet rostral (forwards). Distortions due to different differential enlargement of body parts are apparent, and discontinuities in the representation occur, but the basic orientation of the forelimb digits toward the rostral border of area S1 remains consistent. A smaller cortical area, S11 can be regarded as a smaller, less detailed mirror image of S1.

Except for minor variations in placements of body parts the layout of the somatosensory cortex in most mammals is relatively consistent in appearance. Flying foxes however, show some interesting variations. Firstly, a totally different picture emerges in the orientation and placement of the fore and hind limbs in the map of the flying-fox brain. The relative placement of the forelimb in flying foxes is reversed from the position seen in all other mammals, so that the distal digits extend caudally (backwards) in both cortical areas. This variation appears to reflect the postural differences between flying and walking mammals. The prominent claw of the thumb is at the border of S1 in contrast to its position at the rostral border of the area S1 in other mammals. Moreover, the ventral trunk under the wing is represented rostral to the wing, unlike its representation in other mammals. The dorsal trunk is sparsely represented, and in the area S1 the caudal and rostral position are split into caudomedial and caudolateral cortical locations.

A considerable amount of the flying fox's cortex is devoted to the hairs of the face, indicating that they are important sensory organs. The thumb is also well represented, as is the anterior (back) edge of the propatagium. This indicates the importance of the thumb in its use for climbing, fighting, and grooming. Likewise the anterior wing membrane is important in relaying information on air pressure while flying. The representations of the forelimb and associated wing membrane constitutes over one fifth of area S1.

SPINAL CORD

The spinal cord of bats is characterised by a large cervical enlargement and a small lumbar enlargement. The development of these parts is associated with the large, highly specialised upper extremity (the wings and chest) and the small muscle masses of the lower limb (mainly used for hanging). The most highly developed parts of the spinal cord are the motor columns (serving the nerves related to the wing musculature), the associated spinal ganglia, and the dorsal horns.

EYES AND VISION

Megachiropterans have relatively large, frontally positioned eyes which fix on objects of interest. The eyes and visual system of flying foxes are developed in such a way which greatly assists in the locating of food at night, yet can still operate effectively in full bright sunlight. Many other nocturnal animals close their eyes, or retreat into dark places during daylight hours. Visual acuity tests have shown that in bright light the acuity of flying foxes is not as high as that of a human, but it exceeds that of man at low light levels.

The eyes of megachiropterans are highly adapted for nocturnal vision, being particularly suited to recognising light colours, which is important when searching for food (see Chapter 8). A unique feature of the flying-fox eye is the mosaic of regularly spaced papillae (conical thickenings) that stud the entire inner surface of the choroid (one of the inner layers lining the eye). Although no general consensus has been reached, it would seem that this feature helps in the nutrition of the retina (inner eye), which has no blood vessels of its own, and increases the photosensitive area. The heavily pigmented choroid lies below the light sensitive nervous coat of the retina, and serves to reduce light reflection and penetration. The undulating contour of this studded surface is faithfully matched by the overlying pigment epithelium and photoreceptor layers of the retina, which in flying foxes is 270–300 microns thick.

The pathway taken by images being relayed to the optic part of the brain for interpretation is unusual in flying foxes (Figure 4.9). There is a system of nerve fibres from the retina which cross over from each eye on their way to the optic centres in the brain, with the result that the superior colliculus (where vision is interpreted) on one side of the brain subserves the opposite eye, but only the opposite hemifield of visual space. In all other mammals except primates the cross-over pattern of retinotectal fibres differs from that of the retinothalmic fibres, with the result that the superior colliculus subserves the whole visual field of the opposite eye.

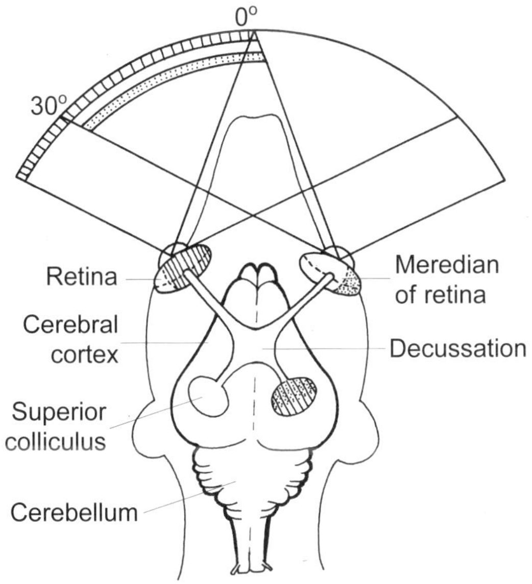

Figure 4.9
A wide overlap of binocular vision and the optic pathway from the eyes to the brain is found only in Megachiroptera and primates. Although information comes from both eyes, it crosses over so that only the opposite side of visual space (cross-hatched) is represented in the visual cortex of the brain. This is in contrast to most other mammals, where the visual input is restricted to the opposite eye. (Modified from Pettigrew *et al*, 1989)

Although primarily nocturnal, the visual prowess of flying foxes extends into bright light conditions — as demonstrated by their high precision of flight and intense visual and social contact at daytime camp sites. This emphasis on a highly developed visual facility in flying foxes is necessary to counterbalance their inability to image their environment acoustically (via echolocation) as do microchiropterans. The visual ability of flying foxes is considered to be equivalent to that of the cat, which is well known for both its diurnal and nocturnal visual alertness.

In daylight, the iris of the eastern tube-nosed fruit bat can be constricted to a pin-hole opening, and there appears to be a flap of tissue which can cover that opening, making the eye light-proof. During the night the iris is dilated to a large opening, which would help in this bat's ability to navigate by sight while flying around the rainforest understorey searching for food. The speed at which this bat can fly in the understorey at night, often with full cloud cover and no moon, navigating by sight alone and dodging vines and other vegetation, is impressive to say the least. Flying foxes will usually refuse to fly in total darkness.

EARS AND HEARING

The ear works as an amplifier to sound that is independent of frequency over the range heard by the animal. Experiments have shown that the auditory representation in the brain of flying foxes (in the inferior colliculus) is quite small, and much smaller than the adjacent visual mid-brain nucleus (superior colliculus).

The external ears of all megachiropterans are simple and relatively small. The ears of tube-nosed fruit bats are short and triangular and have a number of greenish, yellow spots. Each animal has its own distinct pattern of spots. The tragus, which is a prominent flap of skin at the entrance of the ear in microchiropterans, is absent in all megachiropterans. The inner ear of megachiropterans does not show any special modifications, and is similar to most other mammals. Internally, the cochlea, where sound waves are transformed to nervous signals, is relatively small.

The auditory representation in the cortex (see Figure 4.7, page 33) of little red and grey-headed flying foxes is a small region called the inferior colliculus (mid-brain nucleus of central auditory pathway). This suggests that hearing is of minor importance in the flying-fox lifestyle (see 'Vocalisation', page 65). In contrast, the auditory centres of the brain of microchiropterans are generally three to seven times larger than those of megachiropterans.

Audiograms (recordings of what frequencies an animal can hear) for flying foxes show that their hearing is very similar to that of humans (Figure 4.10). The peak sensitivity to sound is around 11 kHz, with a range of 2–40 kHz. The upper frequency limit of mammalian hearing generally shows an inverse relationship with head size. The length of the external ear canal also determines the peak sensitivity in hearing. The upper frequency limit of flying foxes is close to that predicted for that of a mammal with a similar head size. The majority of flying-fox calls have maximum energy in a 4–6 kHz range. Although flying foxes can hear higher frequencies, lower frequency calls are used since the sound will carry further, and will better pass around, rather than be reflected by, small obstacles.

Figure 4.10

Comparison of the audiograms of grey-headed and little red flying foxes with that of a human. The threshold axis is measured in decibels per Sound Pressure Level (SPL). This is a standard measurement of sensitivity where the higher the value the less sensitivity (a louder volume is required to hear that particular frequency). The lack of sensitivity to low frequencies, and those above 30 kHz, by flying foxes, and the better sensitivity of the human ear to low frequencies, are both apparent. (After Calford and McAnally, 1987)

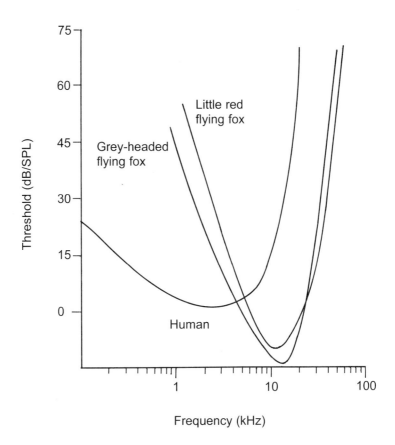

A distinguishing feature of the audiograms of the flying fox is the lack of sensitivity to low and very high frequencies. This has implications in the design of sonic 'scarecrows' used to deter flying foxes considered orchard pests. There have been several models marketed which use ultrasonic blasts at frequencies well above the hearing range of flying foxes, and yet claim to be effective against them.

CHAPTER

REPRODUCTION AND LIFE CYCLE

There are many features of the reproductive system and life cycle of flying foxes that are common to all species. The grey-headed has been observed and researched more than any of the other Australian or overseas flying foxes, and the following refers mainly to this species. Exceptions to the rule are noted in the text, and some individual species, such as *Dobsonia* and the blossom bats, are dealt with at the end of this chapter.

MALE REPRODUCTION

MALE REPRODUCTIVE SYSTEM

The reproductive system of the male flying fox consists of two testes with epididymis and vas deferens, two seminal vesicles and small Cowper's glands. The prostate gland is small. The penis is comparatively long in mature males. Erection of the flying-fox penis is achieved by paired corpora cavenosa (cylindrical structures in the penis) being engorged with blood. These are fused for much of their length, and have many partitions. The small baculum in the tip of the penis caps the distal end of the corpora cavenosa. The testes descend into the scrotum for most of the breeding season, but the visibility of a scrotum varies with the animal's behaviour and air temperature.

Plate 1
The Black flying fox (*Pteropus alecto*) can be found from northern NSW, around the northern coast of Australia to mid Western Australia. It frequently shares its camp site with other species of flying foxes. (Theo Allofs)

Plate 3a
During the day, grey-headed flying foxes (*Pteropus poliocephalus*) often hang on a branch with their wings wrapped around their body. (Theo Allofs)

Plate 3b
This specimen of the grey-headed flying fox (*Pteropus polio-cephalus*) shows the characteristic grey head, orange collar and hairy lower legs of the species. (Clancy Hall)

Plate 3c (opposite)
The grey-headed flying fox (*Pteropus poliocephalus*) is restricted to south-east coastal Australia from Bundaberg to Melbourne, and has camps in the suburban areas of Brisbane, Sydney and Melbourne. (Theo Allofs)

Plate 4 (opposite)
The spectacled flying fox (*Pteropus conspicillatus*) inhabits the wet tropics of Queensland where it feeds mainly on rainforest fruit. The species is also found in New Guinea.
(Theo Allofs)

Plate 5 (top)
In Australia, the large-eared flying fox (*Pteropus macrotis*) has been found only on Boigu Island in the Torres Strait, close to the New Guinea mainland. The species is widespread along southern coastal New Guinea and is likely to be found on other Torres Strait islands.
(Les Hall)

Plate 6 (bottom)
The Torresian flying fox (*Pteropus banakrisi*) has been only recently found on Moa Island in the Torres Strait. It is similar in external appearance to the black flying fox but is smaller, has proportionately longer ears and feet, and a different dentition.
(Noel Chopping)

Plate 7
The bare-backed flying fox (*Dobsonia magna*), so named because its wings are joined along the middle of its back making the bat appear to have a naked back, is also found in New Guinea where this photograph was taken. (Steve Donnellan)

Plate 8
The facial features of the eastern tube-nosed fruit bat (*Nyctimene robinsoni*) make identification of the species easy, and the pattern of yellow patches on bare skin of the ear and nose area is distinct for each individual. (Jack Pettigrew)

Plate 9
This is the only photo of an unidentified species of tube-nosed fruit bat (*Nyctimene* sp.) from Moa Island in the Torres Strait. The taxonomy of the Nyctimene group of fruit bats is at present under revision, and it is likely that this species is widespread in New Guinea. It has not been previously recorded in Australia.
(Les Hall)

Plate 10
The Queensland blossom bat (*Syconycteris australis*) frequents heathlands and coastal swamps from northern NSW to Cape York. During the day it roosts in dense vegetation and at night emerges to feed on the nectar of Banksias and Melaleucas.
(Les Hall)

Plate 11
The northern blossom bat (*Macroglossus minimus*) has a longer, more pointed nose than the similar eastern blossom bat, allowing it better access to nectar in tubular flowers. This bat has a wide distribution, from northern coastal Australia, through the Indonesian Islands, to South-East Asia. (Les Hall)

Plate 12
At this camp at Woodend in Ipswich, south-east Queensland, black, grey-headed and little red flying foxes share the one camp site. Little reds with their characteristic semi-transparent wings can be seen flying past a group of grey-headed flying foxes hanging in the trees. (Theo Allofs)

Plate 13
Most of the large flying foxes like these grey-headed flying foxes hang on branches, roughly one body space apart from each other. This spacing can be influenced by the time of year when mating occurs or when females have large semi-independent young.
(Patrina Birt)

Plate 14
In contrast to other species of flying foxes (see Plate 13), little reds frequently crowd closely together when roosting. One or two animals in the centre can support up to twenty flying foxes. A number of these roosting groups can weigh a considerable amount, causing even large branches to break under the combined weight.
(Les Hall)

Plate 15
The evening exodus of flying foxes from their daytime camp is always an impressive sight. Some species have been recorded travelling 40 kilometres to a food source and returning to their camp on the same night. (Les Hall)

Plate 16 (below left)
Flying fox camps are frequently located beside prominent watercourses which are probably used as navigation aids. Continuous occupation of the same site over a number of years, such as this one in south-east Queensland, results in damage to the vegetation. The brown coloured area in the centre of the photograph is actually flying foxes roosting on bare limbs. (Les Hall)

Plate 17 (below right)
As towns grow and forest resources decrease along the eastern Australian coast, flying foxes are becoming more urbanised. This camp site in Brisbane shows how close some camps are to houses. Up to 5000 black and grey-headed flying foxes can squeeze into the vegetation shown in the centre of the photograph. During summer the camp is often used by nomadic little reds who swell the population to 25 000 flying foxes. (Les Hall)

Plate 18 (left)
The wings of a flying fox make an effective raincoat. This little red flying fox, tucked in under its wings, seems unperturbed by an afternoon shower. (Theo Allofs)

Plate 19 (right)
To urinate or defecate, flying foxes hang head-up by their thumbs, do their job, and then return to hanging upside-down after they have finished. (Theo Allofs)

Plate 20 (opposite)
Most flying foxes mate in the camp during the day. These little red flying foxes are displaying a typical mating posture, with the female at the front and the male at the rear. (Theo Allofs)

Plate 21 (above left)
Flying foxes spend a lot of time grooming their fur and wings. This little red flying fox is licking its wing clean prior to spreading an oily substance from glands on its nose onto the wing surface to help waterproof and keep the wing membrane soft. (Theo Allofs)

Plate 22 (above right)
In southern and eastern Australia little red flying foxes are nomadic and follow the flowering of eucalypts and other forest trees. They frequently 'drop in' on camp sites occupied by other species of flying fox and remain there until local flowering has finished. (Theo Allofs)

Plate 23 (top left)

Damage to the vegetation in flying fox camps can be severe if the camp area is too small to allow the movement of flying foxes around the camp site. This is particularly noticeable in small camps when an influx of migratory flying foxes arrives. Long-term occupied flying-fox camps have sufficient vegetation in the camp area to allow movement of the bats away to new trees when old trees become damaged.
(Theo Allofs)

Plate 24 (top right)

A characteristic feature of little red flying foxes is their habit of clumping together when roosting on a branch. This occurs at any time during the year, on hot or cold days.
(Theo Allofs)

Plate 25 (centre)

Most grey-headed flying foxes can be identified by their individual characteristic features which include sex, body size, length of fur, and colour of the fur on the back and on the head.
(Theo Allofs)

Plate 26 (bottom)

In the wet tropics of northern Queensland flying foxes are important seed dispersers and pollinators of many rainforest trees. This spectacled flying fox has pollen grains on its muzzle after feeding on black bean flowers.
(Theo Allofs)

The acrosome (the membrane at the head of sperm responsible for penetrating the ovum) of flying foxes has two lateral spikes on each side that extend approximately to the same width on the head in the region of the equatorial or middle segment. While these barbs could serve to stabilise or anchor the apical segment of the acrosome, they could provide some specific mechanical role in penetration of the zona pellucida (outer protective covering) of the female egg and protect more caudal structures from abrasive damage. It is also possible that a large acrosome may be related to sperm competitiveness and selection pressure 'rewarding' spermatozoa with a high enzyme content (for release during the process of fertilisation). These acrosomal spikes are also seen in the sperm of the microchiropteran genera *Rhinolophus* and *Miniopterus*. Among other mammalian orders, a protruding apical segment to the acrosome is only seen in the Cetaceans (whales and dolphins) and the Insectivora.

In male bare-backed flying foxes there are two pairs of scent glands. One extends from the base of the ear downward and forward to the angle of the mouth, and the other is near the junction of the wing-membrane with the body. These glands produce a musky odour and are also responsible for the brown stains on the walls of their roost sites under large boulders.

MALE BREEDING CYCLE

Male puberty begins in the second breeding season after birth but they do not achieve effective fertility until the third breeding season, that is at about an age of 30 months. In adult males the production of sperm reaches a peak in February/March, and epididymal sperm content is maximum in April. Both fall rapidly to a minimum in June. Peripheral levels of plasma testosterone also rise sharply in January to a peak in March. Hormone levels then decline rapidly for the rest of the year. The little red flying fox's cycle is offset six months compared to other species, and its peak mating period is in November and December.

The testis starts to grow in September with the increasing day length, with further growth occurring in December, reaching its greatest size in February and March. By then the testes have descended fully into the scrotum, which is then on constant display. The seminiferous cycle of flying foxes is only about 16 days, similar to that of humans.

The major accessory glands, the seminal vesicles, also grow during the breeding season until April. From February to April, the epithelial cells enlarge and bud off their apical tips into the lumen of the gland, where they are stored to form a large component of the semen. The glands regress rapidly in May and are non-secretory from June to December.

FEMALE REPRODUCTION

Female flying foxes are seasonal breeders and produce one young per year. Most of the year is tied up with some part of their reproductive cycle or caring for young.

FEMALE REPRODUCTIVE SYSTEM

In female flying foxes there are two ovaries which have a thick capsule. The primordial follicles are restricted to the caudal (front) pole of the ovary and ovulation can occur from either ovary. Ovarian follicles and the corpus luteum do not protrude above the surface. The oviducts empty into a bicornuate uterus. There is an unusual arrangement with the ovarian artery, which is only seen in the Megachiroptera. The artery is coiled and enclosed within in a venus sinus (an artery inside a vein). The vagina undergoes changes in response to sex hormones, and a female's reproductive state can be determined precisely from vaginal smears.

There is an asymmetric development of the endometrium (the lining of the uterus) following fertilisation. This local endometrial reaction of thickened tissue is always on the same side as the ovary that released the ovum.

FEMALE BREEDING CYCLE

Female flying foxes do not commence to breed until the second breeding season after their birth. Ovaries contain large secondary follicles from January to March. Sperm is not usually found in females, denoting mating, until March. The act of mating itself does not induce follicle maturation or ovulation.

Copulation can be a short torrid affair but often it is a more involved procedure and can last up to 20 minutes (see below). Multiple matings in one day, or over several days, are normal. Most mating is done with the nearby dominant male in the camp, but instances of females mating with a number of males over several days have been observed. Female receptivity is not tightly linked with female sex hormone levels. It is possible that female flying foxes are similar to female humans and become receptive and acquiesce following courtship, while coition is determined by male behaviour, drive, perseverance, and perhaps pheromones.

Females ovulate from late February to April, and implantation occurs on the opposite side of the uterus from the side where the egg was shed. Births occur from late September until November, but have been recorded in all months of the year. Female little red flying foxes give birth in May and June. Lactation lasts for about six weeks (or up to several months in captivity) and following its cessation, females can again become receptive to males.

FLYING-FOX LIFE CYCLES

COURTING AND COPULATION

During the rearing of young (September to January) most males roost away from females, either in groups or scattered around the camp. In February and March the males commence to isolate themselves and establish a display area on a horizontal branch. They become aggressive and defend the area vigorously. Males mark their territory by rubbing their shoulders (where the scapular gland is located) and muzzle along a branch and usually patrol a metre each side of where they hang.

Vocalisations in the camp reach a peak during this period and no bats seem to get any daytime sleep. Males who have established a territory regularly groom and display their genitals by licking them. They often have a partial erection. Gradually, as young leave their mothers, females come back into ovulation and are attracted to the marked area, after which they hang nearby. Females will join in territorial disputes and help drive off an interposing male.

Males investigate females by first sniffing, with an outstretched posture, her scapular and genital areas. Females with large young still in tow reject the males by vocalising, biting or flapping their wings. If the female tolerates the male's advances, a grooming session commences, which can last up to half an hour. When investigating a female, the male sniffs at her genital area with his ears held back. If the female is receptive he licks the vaginal opening. Occasionally the female initiates precopulatory behaviour by wrapping her wing and legs around the male so that he supports her completely. She repeats this until the male begins to lick her genital area or begins mutual grooming.

Most copulations occur in March and April, although attempted copulations and homosexual activity have been seen in all months of the year. Copulation is performed dorso-ventrally, with the male holding the female's wing between her upper arm and his forearm, and gripping the back of her neck with his teeth (plate 20). The male may also hold the female against his body with the claws of one leg which grips the female's abdomen. The penis is very flexible and can be moved independently of pelvic movements. After copulation each partner grooms the genital area and then the rest of the body surface. Intromission can last from ten seconds to several minutes, and up to four copulations in one hour have been observed in one pair of flying foxes.

WINTER

In April, when mating has almost ceased, flying fox camps become noticeably quieter. Pregnancy lasts about six months, and during this time females congregate into groups where individuals hang close to each other and indulge in mutual grooming. Males become less aggressive as winter approaches, and they cease to defend their territories and return to mixed groups. Individual animals frequently move away to other camp sites. Winter months can be hard times for flying foxes, particularly if there is poor flowering and cold, windy weather. Mortality of young bats is high at this time, especially if covering long distances is necessary to find reliable food. It appears that experience and learning where to find reliable food are critical for flying fox survival.

BIRTHING

Observations of birthing behaviour have been made on black and grey-headed flying foxes, both in captivity and in the wild, and the following relates to these species.

Prior to the birth of young, the sexes tend to segregate, with groups of females hanging close together. Nearby, and usually on a branch above, will be one or two males. Squabbling is only mild and occurs when private space is invaded. Females often sniff each other, but male investigations of females provoke vocalisation, cuffing with the thumb claw, and biting.

Birth occurs during daylight hours. When birth is imminent females hang by their feet and often by a thumb as well. The genital area is vigorously licked and the newborn appears head first. The head of the young is expelled and there is a pause in the proceedings. This can last from ten minutes up to several hours with just the head of the young poking out of the mother. Its eyes are open and its ears twitch. The young generally remains silent until totally delivered, but may yawn or occasionally call.

When the young is fully expelled it clings immediately to its mother's chest. In microchiropterans the uropatagium, a membrane which connects the two hind legs to the tail, is used to receive the expelled newborn as the female turns head up. This membrane is absent in flying foxes, and females hang by their feet and claws to form a U-shaped body sling supported by her feet and thumbs during the birth process, and manoeuvres the newborn to a teat located in the wing pit with a combination of licking or grasping with a spare thumb or foot. The umbilical cord is chewed off and shortly afterwards the placenta is ejected and eaten.

The newborn commences to vocalise with short, high-pitched calls immediately after birth. Newborn young have disproportionately large feet and their mouths have a set of deeply curved milk teeth for attaching to the teat. There is also a hook-like growth on the inside of the thumb claw which facilitates a grip on the mother's fur. The young stays closely attached to its mother for the first two or three weeks.

MATERNAL AND INFANT BEHAVIOUR

The belly of the young is only lightly furred and this allows transfer of the mother's body heat. Mothers frequently wrap their wings around their young for the first week or so, and hold them close to their body. For the first three weeks the unco-ordinated young is carried on its mother during her foraging flights at night.

By three weeks the young becomes too heavy to carry and it is left in a creche with other young in the centre of the camp at night while the mother goes out to feed. As the young gets older, it remains on the branch where its mother roosts during the day. Three-week-old young do not appear to recognise their own mother and will grab any female nearby. Mothers, on the other hand, recognise their own young, more than likely through olfactory cues.

After a month the young becomes more co-ordinated, and crawls around its mother and will hang separately beside her. It commences to groom itself, its ears flick and it is very alert both visually and acoustically. It will react to a perceived threat by opening its wings.

By about six weeks, the young has grown to adult proportions and does a lot of wing flapping while hanging beside its mother. In its second month, the young still spends a lot of time hanging on its mother. It climbs in the vegetation near its mother and chews on leaves and twigs. It flaps its wings regularly. At night the mother leaves the young behind when she go out to feed.

Initially the young are all left in a central area of the camp which can be identified by their high pitched calls. Mothers often have trouble leaving young behind when they fly off to feed. Young bats will cling desperately to their mothers' nipples with their curved milk teeth, and hang on to branches with their toe claws when their mothers try to fly away. As a result, the length of a nursing mother's nipple is elongated (which may be reliably used for identifying such females).

Depending on the distance and quality of food, females return during the night or just before dawn and locate their young in the creche. Often a number of young from the group will attempt to attach themselves to one incoming female, and she will fly off, circle around calling, and land again. Once the correct young attaches itself to her, she flies off to her regular roosting area in the camp.

A young bat can fly at three months and commences to leave the camp on short forays. It still suckles from its mother, but has lost its milk teeth. The young flies around the camp at dusk, crashing into trees on landing, and then calls to its mother. The mother returns the call and the young flies back to her.

In January and February young flying foxes form small groups in the camp. They often hang near a large adult and remain as a group until winter. Groups of young bats can be seen flying out of the camp.

They do not have the purposeful direction of the adults, and are reminiscent of a group of school kids going home from school and exploring their environment. Progress is slow as they carry out aerial bombs on each other, explore vegetation and duck from imaginary predators. It is probable that these groups do not initially go far from the camp, and that the trips serve as navigational training.

Observations have been made on the schooling of young flying foxes following the release of orphan young from human carers. It appears that adult males first shepherd groups of recently independent young. These adults warn the young of impending predators and escort them on their initial group foraging expeditions.

Young still roost near their mothers after four months, and are occasionally carried by their mothers if the camp is disturbed. Mothers often groom their young, mainly by licking, particularly in the genital area. Mother/young bonds are known to persist up to six years in semi-captive animals.

When adult females become receptive to males and mating occurs in late February and March, the adult males involved in schooling of young lose interest and turn their attention to adult females. By this time the young are independent and forage in small groups or by themselves. It is important for there to be a reliable food supply near the camp for the survival of young.

Females do not mate until the second breeding season after their birth. Although they show evidence of sperm production earlier, captive young males do not become effectively fertile until their third year.

SPECIES VARIATIONS

As noted above, the little red flying fox has a major difference in that it breeds six months out of phase with the other flying foxes. Its young are born in May: the other species mostly have their young in October and November.

There is very little detailed information on the reproduction and life history of the cave-dwelling bare-backed flying fox. Males mature at about two years and copulation occurs at the end of the wet season in May and June. A single young is born between September and November and is carried by its mother for about a month and nursed for a further four to five months. When roosting in boulder piles, there appear to be small cohesive groups which could represent social units. Based on body size variations, these groups appear to be composed of representatives of different age groups.

In the northern parts of its range, the Queensland blossom bat breeds throughout the year. In more southern parts, in New South

Wales, there are two birth periods: one young is born in October or November; and another between February and April. Lactation lasts up to three months.

Northern blossom bat births generally occur in the dry season, just prior to the wet. In South-East Asian rainforest, this bat is known to be a continuous breeder. Male northern blossom bats have a raised V-shaped chest gland that resembles a welt. They produce a pungent odour that is musky and penetrating and probably originates from this gland. Females and juveniles lack this distinctive gland and smell.

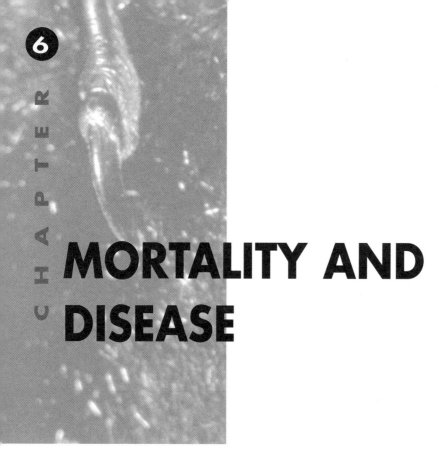

MORTALITY AND DISEASE

In captivity flying foxes can live for over 30 years, but there is no accurate data for longevity in the wild. Using growth rings in teeth, it is estimated that animals over 20 years exist in populations of black and grey-headed flying foxes. There is some evidence that flying foxes continue to grow in body size for the whole of their life. Older animals are characterised by their worn teeth, scarred wings and ears, and gingerish tips to their fur. These animals always have larger body dimensions.

MORTALITY

There is very little information on the overall age structure of megachiropteran populations, or age-related mortality rates. Their generally long life span and low reproductive rate indicate that flying foxes have had an evolutionary history involving low natural mortality rates.

BIRTH ABNORMALITIES

There is an increasing number of cases of abnormalities in newborn flying foxes. The abnormalities most commonly seen are cranio-facial and fluid on the brain (hydrocephaly, hydranencephaly, and porancephaly), and involve cleft palate and an enlarged cranium. Several cases of supernumery digits (polydactyly) have also been recorded where there were two thumbs on one wing, and others had been recorded with seven toes.

In some years the incidence of abnormalities can be 1 in 100 young brought in for human care. Most of these young have trouble feeding, particularly ones with cleft palates, and do not survive. There is some indication that mothers often abandon young with severe abnormalities. Birth abnormalities are more common in black flying foxes, but have been recorded in grey-headed and spectacled flying foxes as well. In some localities (for instance Brisbane and the Atherton Tableland) these abnormalities can have a significant impact on the mortality rates of newborn animals.

The cause or causes of these abnormalities have not been determined. Similar birth abnormalities in other animals can be caused by a number of chemicals or compounds. Abnormalities result from females ingesting or being exposed to these substances at an early stage of their pregnancy. Plant alkaloids are one of the substances known to cause such abnormalities.

The number of birth abnormalities in flying foxes varies greatly from year to year, suggesting that the cause could be related to periods of natural food shortage. These shortages result in flying foxes feeding on fruit which is still developing and which often contain alkaloids as a natural deterrent to feeding, or on plants not normally eaten and which contain substances causing abnormalities. Such feeding practices often occur in late winter and early spring — a time which has become a notorious period for food shortage with flying foxes, and when females are in an early stage of pregnancy. Low levels of folic acid in the diet of females in early stages of pregnancy is also known to cause cleft palates in newborn young, and it is possible that the normally available dietary source of folic acid has become unreliable in these cases.

Mass die-offs

In 1978 in a camp near Beenleigh there was a mass abortion of close to full-term foetuses of the grey-headed flying fox. Several thousand females (out of approximately 12 000) lost their young which were expelled complete with the placenta and festooned the branches of the understorey of the camp. Crows and foxes were feeding on the carcasses.

It is possible that a bacterium, parasite or disease could have caused the mass abortion. A similar mass abortion of near full-term young was seen at the Indooroopilly Island camp of grey-headed flying foxes in Brisbane in 1983. Epidemics of unknown origin and pathogen have occurred and have severely depleted populations of flying foxes on the Caroline, Fiji, Admiralty and Solomon islands. On these islands mortality rates were extremely high, and it is thought that the responsible agent was introduced by humans or domestic animals, rather than being a natural occurrence.

A post-breeding die-off of males has been recorded in captive little red flying foxes. It is thought that their immune system is depressed from high hormone levels during the mating season, thus making them more susceptible to pathogens.

High mortality may also occur when weather conditions are wet, windy and cold at the end of winter. There is a lack of natural food and the available nectar is greatly diluted by rain. Flying foxes seem to be too weak to fly to areas where more food is available. This happened in a wide area of far north-eastern New South Wales and south-eastern Queensland in 1991, and in the Brisbane area in the previous year. Both instances coincided with adverse weather conditions. In the Brisbane district over a thousand dead flying foxes were reported following a radio request for information. Judged on body size and tooth wear, many of these were one- or two-year-old juveniles.

Continuous high air temperature of over 40°C causes death from heat stress in flying foxes. Smoke from bushfires seems to stupefy them and they fly aimlessly around their camp. Many flying foxes are killed when a fire goes through or close to a camp site, but it is not known if deaths are from smoke inhalation or directly from the heat of the fire.

MAN-MADE OBSTACLES

Power lines and aerial wires are responsible for the death and injury of thousands of flying foxes yearly, and in some parts of north-east Australia the presence of a rotting flying fox carcass on power lines is an everyday sight. Frequently the electrocutions are on power lines near fruiting or flowering trees. The peak time for electrocutions is during summer storms when females are pregnant or carrying young. Local power authorities have come to the rescue and are now putting protective aerial bundle cabling on wires where frequent flying-fox electrocutions occur.

Flying foxes, particularly little reds, are prone to catching their wings on the top strand of barbed-wire fences. These fences are frequently obvious and are out in quite open paddocks. Little red flying foxes are known to fly low over the ground or water when flying into a breeze, and this is a possible reason for them being found on fences only a metre or so off the ground. Several tube-nosed fruit bats have also been found caught on barbed-wire fences. (See Chapter 11 for removal and care instructions for barbed-wire fence victims.)

Figure 6.1
Flying foxes,
particularly little
reds, often fly close
to the ground and
become entangled
on the top strand of
barbed-wire fences.
Unable to free
themselves, they
die a slow death.
(Les Hall)

Flying foxes can pose a serious threat to small aircraft near airports at dusk. The body of a flying fox causes serious damage if sucked into the engine of a jet aircraft. A little red flying fox was scraped out of the fibreglass nose cone of an American Airforce B52 bomber which had been on exercises over Cape York. Despite claims to the contrary, it is unlikely that the little red was flying at a high altitude. Australian F-111 fighter bombers have struck flying foxes at 100 metres when on exercises involving low altitude flying, causing serious engine damage.

The catamaran travelling from Urangan to Fraser Island frequently collides with little red flying foxes. Weather conditions seem to be the causative factor. Strong winds and rain force the bats to fly at 2–3 metres above sea level, and they crash into the upper deck of the catamaran, frequently being killed.

LEAD POISONING

Lead toxicity is a common cause of poisoning in animals throughout the world. The source of the lead causing the poison is generated by various manufacturing processes, and its addition to petrol.

Flying foxes have been shown to be good indicators of lead in the environment. Animals showing signs of lead poisoning have poor body condition, muscle myopathy (that is, they will fall off their perch), dull eyes, and diarrhoea. When tested, such bats show extremely high lead levels in their body tissues and fur. The high levels of lead in the fur suggest that it could be either primary contamination from lead in the atmosphere or secondary contamination from contact with or eating vegetation where lead has settled. Fortunately, lead toxicity in flying foxes seems to have decreased markedly since unleaded petrol was introduced in Australia.

CULLING OF FLYING FOXES

Culling of flying foxes has been conducted in various ways for more than a century, and in the 1800s there was a government bounty paid to encourage the practice. Culling took place both in orchards, where flying foxes were regarded as pests, and at their camp sites. There are records of barrels of scrap metal and gelignite being hauled into the tree tops of camps and exploded. This disgusting and totally inhumane method of control left many live animals maimed and injured. Fortunately it is a thing of the past.

Culling is today an illegal activity without the required permit. Illegal killing still arises when fruit growers exceed the number of animals specified on their culling permit, or do not apply for a permit to kill flying foxes. A study on the animals killed on the New South Wales permit system estimated that in the seven years from 1986 to 1992, permits were allocated to cull over 240 000 flying foxes. It also showed that these licensed people were only one half of those actually culling flying foxes, indicating the extent of the illegal practice, and that many more flying foxes were actually killed.

During recent trials on a new flying fox deterrent system in orchards in northern New South Wales, it was established that most orchardists would cull approximately 20–30 flying foxes each night during the harvest season. The harvest season lasts about six weeks, and the orchardists cull every night of the week: this equates to 840–1260 flying foxes killed per orchard per season. When this is further multiplied by the total number of orchards over a large area, it is obvious that culling has to be regarded as a significant mortality factor. Combined with the significant loss of its winter foraging habitat, culling has contributed to the serious decline of the grey-headed flying fox.

It is unfortunate that for many years there has been an impasse between people culling flying foxes and wildlife biologists seeking information on the animals killed. Information on population structure and other aspects of flying-fox dynamics — which could have been collected from flying-fox bodies following the massive culls at camps — could have been used to formulate a properly designed management plan for flying foxes.

PREDATORS

Flying foxes have to contend with a diverse range of predators which vary from reptiles to birds of prey and mammals.

The stomach content of crocodiles shows that these reptiles regularly catch flying foxes. Two capture techniques are used by crocodiles. One involves the crocodile floating, mostly submerged under the water surface, in the middle of rivers and estuaries. When flying foxes glide down to drink in the evening, the crocodile snaps them up as they dip into the surface of the water. The second technique involves crocodiles thrashing amongst mangroves with their tails in an effort to dislodge and panic flying foxes roosting low down near the water.

Snakes, particularly the large pythons, frequently prey on flying foxes, and most permanent flying-fox camps have their resident python. These snakes climb trees and appear to mesmerise the flying foxes. The pythons grab the flying foxes and quickly crush the body, which is then swallowed whole, head first.

White-bellied sea eagles (*Haliaeetus leucogaster*) and Brahminy kites (*Haliastur indus*) continually patrol flying fox camps in coastal areas. These birds have been seen attacking roosting flying foxes, and freshly killed flying foxes have been found under their feeding roosts. Whistling (*Haliastur sphenurus*) and black kites (*Milvus migrans*) search for dead or dying individuals in flying-fox camps. Crows (*Corvus* spp.) also scavenge around flying-fox camps, and help remove dead or dying animals.

The food of powerful owls (*Ninox strenua*) in the Brisbane area includes both black and grey-headed flying foxes. These owls are nocturnal hunters and appear to prey on the flying foxes feeding on eucalypt blossoms, rather than preying on them at camp sites.

Dingoes, domestic dogs and foxes have been seen in and around flying-fox camps. It is possible that they are looking for dead individuals, but with the low roosting habit of little reds, it is possible that they could catch live flying foxes.

Little is known about the predators of fruit and blossom bats. Since they roost in foliage, it is likely that tree snakes could be potential predators.

PARASITES

All megachiropterans carry parasites of some sort, both internally or externally.

The ascaridoid nematode (a round worm), *Toxocara pteropodis*, is found in all Australian mainland flying-fox species. Worm infections develop only in suckling juveniles, with a prevalence exceeding 50 per cent. Contamination of the roost environment with *Toxocara* eggs over summer leads to the infection of most adult bats, which harbour third-stage larvae in their livers. In females, larvae move internally to mammary glands after parturition to infect offspring through the milk. Infected juveniles rarely harbour more than three or four of these large (up to 15 centimetres long) worms, which are expelled spontaneously prior to weaning at about five months of age.

Eggs and body segments of another type of parasitic worm, a hymenolepid cestode, have been found in the intestines of adult and juvenile little red, and juvenile black and grey-headed flying foxes. The significance of this worm in flying-fox ecology is unknown.

Small, long-legged, brownish insects seen scurrying around in the fur of megachiropterans are parasitic wingless flies. They are from the family Nycteribiidae, and two species are found on Australian flying foxes. *Cyclopodia albertisii* is usually found on larger flying foxes, such as the black and grey-headed, and *C. australis* on the smaller little red flying fox.

The female nycteribiid leaves its roosting host to deposit a full-term prepupa near the roost site. The prepupa is extruded and affixed to leaves or branches with an adhesive secretion. The pale maggot-like prepupa then changes into a pupa covered with a dark protective shell. When it hatches as a fly, it climbs back onto a flying fox. For these wingless flies to breed successfully, their bat hosts must occupy the roost site for extended periods of time to allow the newly emerged flies to find a suitable host. These wingless flies feed on dead skin cells and do not directly harm their hosts. It is possible that they are a positive stimulus for grooming the fur, but they may also be involved as vectors of pathogens.

There is a variety of mites which inhabit different locations on the skin, wing membranes and the fur of megachiropterans. Blood-sucking spinturnicid mites of the genus *Meristaspis* are common on flying foxes, and will also transfer onto human skin. At least three sarcoptid mite species occur on Australian flying foxes.

The paralysis tick, *Ixodes holocyclus*, is occasionally seen on grey-headed flying foxes around Brisbane, and on the Atherton Tableland this tick is responsible for the paralysis and deaths of many spectacled flying foxes. The tick, mainly found on pregnant or lactating females, reach peak numbers from October to December. How and why the tick gets onto the flying foxes has not been established. Only certain camps of spectacled flying foxes are infected, and it appears that outbreaks at these sites were unknown before 1990. It is possible that a change in foraging behaviour, caused by the extensive clearing in some areas, has resulted in the flying foxes becoming exposed to the tick. The viability of spectacled flying-fox camps on the Atherton Tableland is under serious threat if the infestations of *Ixodes* continue.

DISEASES IN FLYING FOXES

Flying foxes are subjected to a wide variety of pathogens and frequently carry a number of antibodies for diseases that also affect humans. Antibodies for Ross River virus, Murray Valley encephalitis, and Leptospirosus have been found in grey-headed, black, and spectacled flying foxes. While the presence of antibodies indicates that flying foxes have been exposed to these viruses, there is no indication that flying foxes are important in the spread of these diseases to humans. A study in Queensland showed that there was no relationship between outbreaks of Ross River virus in humans and the presence of flying-fox camps.

Besides those mentioned above, two viruses previously unrecognised in Australian flying foxes were discovered in 1996. These do have implications for human health.

HENDRA

The Hendra story began in 1994 when there were two outbreaks of a disease which was fatal to humans and horses. The outbreaks occurred within one month of each other, but were 800 kilometres apart, one in Brisbane and the other in Mackay. In the Brisbane suburb of Hendra, 21 horses were infected, of which 14 died or were put down. Two people were also infected, one of whom died. At Mackay, two horses died, and a person died of relapsing encephalitis 12 months later. The name Equine Morbillivirus (EMV) was first proposed for the virus isolated from these cases, but subsequent studies showed that the new virus was distinct from the morbilliviruses — and it has since been named Hendra virus.

Since Hendra virus was similar to a group of viruses usually found in wildlife, a search began for an animal species which was present at Brisbane and Mackay, and which could move between these two localities. Although there was no direct evidence that flying foxes moved between Brisbane and Mackay, large scale movements of little red flying foxes were known to occur in south-east Queensland. Blood was collected from flying foxes, as well as from a large number of other wildlife species including possums and bandicoots, by the Queensland

Department of Primary Industries. In the initial study 5000 blood samples were taken from 46 species of wildlife, and antibodies against Hendra virus were found only in flying foxes. The presence of antibodies in flying foxes' blood indicated that they had been exposed to Hendra virus.

Since then, hundreds of flying foxes, including all four mainland species, have been tested. The results showed that about 14 per cent carried antibodies to Hendra virus. However blood tests on people who have had close contact with flying foxes, such as animal carers and researchers, have shown no sign of Hendra virus antibodies in their blood. This indicates that flying foxes are an unlikely source of infection for humans. It is significant that the two people who died from Hendra virus both became infected after being exposed to horses with the virus.

In early 1999, a third case of Hendra virus was reported from a horse kept in an urban area near Cairns. The horse died within two days of it first showing symptoms of illness. There appears to be a pattern emerging in horse fatalities from Hendra virus. They were all well bred and cared for horses located in urban or near urban areas. All outbreaks have been in coastal Queensland and within the distributional range of the black flying fox. But despite a considerable effort, the link between flying foxes, Hendra virus, and horses has not been established. It appears that a certain event, or chain of events, which may involve pregnant animals, is necessary for the transmission of the virus from flying foxes to horses. Research is continuing on this intriguing and extremely important virus.

LYSSAVIRUS

In May 1996 a sick black flying fox from Ballina, on the New South Wales central coast, was sent in for pathological testing. The bat was unable to fly and had mild tremors. It was put down, and tests on its brain and other nervous tissue revealed what was first thought to be the Rabies virus. It was subsequently called Australian bat Lyssavirus.

In September 1996, Australian bat Lyssavirus was isolated from the uterine fluid of a female grey-headed flying fox which had aborted her young after being caught on a barbed-wire fence. Since these initial findings, Australian bat Lyssavirus has also been isolated from little red flying foxes, as well as an insectivorous microchiropteran, the yellow-bellied bat (*Saccolaimus flaviventris*). All animals that had the virus were sick and showed signs of nervous disorders, such as tremors, paralysis and aggressive behaviour. Antibodies for Australian bat Lyssavirus have recently been found in another microchiropteran, the long-eared bat (*Nyctophilus* sp.). It is now known that there are two separate strains of Australian bat

Lyssavirus, one carried by megachiropterans and the other by microchiropterans. As yet, Australian bat Lyssavirus has not been found in South or Western Australia, but bats from these states have not been fully evaluated.

In November 1996 a fauna rehabilitator from Rockhampton died in Royal Brisbane Hospital from neurological problems caused by Australian bat Lyssavirus. This person had recently been bitten and scratched by a variety of animals, including black and little red flying foxes, and a sick yellow-bellied bat. Unfortunately the bats that had bitten the carer had in the meantime been released back into the wild and it was assumed that her death was due to one of the flying-fox bites. Subsequent extensive sampling of flying foxes in the Rockhampton area failed to find any trace of the megachiropteran strain of Australian bat Lyssavirus. A number of sick and dead yellow-bellied bats which had been handed in for testing were then found to have the slightly different, microchiropteran, strain of the virus. Further testing of specimens kept from the Rockhampton fatality revealed that the virus which was responsible for her death was the microchiropteran strain — which had come from the yellow-bellied bat, not from a flying fox as was earlier thought.

In December 1998, another wildlife carer, this time from Mackay, died from neurological problems caused by Australian bat Lyssavirus. This person had been bitten by a flying fox two years prior to her death, but had not taken the post-exposure Rabies injections as a precautionary measure. In this case it has been established that it was the megachiropteran strain of Australian bat Lyssavirus which was responsible for her death. This is the first and only recorded human death from Australian bat Lyssavirus inflicted by a flying fox, and is the reason why health authorities regard flying foxes as a very low public health risk.

Rabies has been well studied overseas, but Australia is the only continent where it is absent. Because they are so similar, Lyssavirus behaviour is expected to act in the same way as Rabies. These viruses affect the nervous system. Following its introduction into the body of an animal, usually by a bite, the virus travels through the peripheral nervous system to the spinal cord, then to the brain, where it multiplies before moving to the ducts of the salivary glands. In the brain, the virus causes severe neurological problems which result in the animal suffering partial paralysis, tremors, altered metabolism and aggression. The virus combines with saliva in the salivary gland and can be transferred to another animal during biting, and the process starts all over again. Lyssavirus is so closely related to Rabies that the easily obtainable immunisation against Rabies will protect a person from Lyssavirus.

First aid against flying-fox bites

If any person, even if previously vaccinated, is bitten or scratched by any flying fox, even if apparently healthy, you should:

- Immediately wash the wound thoroughly with soapy water and apply appropriate dressings.
- Contact the local veterinarian, hospital or public health authority. These will probably recommend a post-exposure Rabies vaccination, which should be carried out as soon as possible.
- If at all possible (without putting anyone else at risk) the bat should be captured and submitted for testing. Again the local public health authority will advise how to arrange to have this done.

Flying foxes that look sick or injured, or which have attacked cats or dogs, should also be submitted for testing to the appropriate local health authority, or Department of Agriculture or Primary Industries.

People handling flying foxes in any way — be it research, rehabilitation, raising orphan young, or for wildlife display — should be protected against Australian bat Lyssavirus. This can be achieved by having a course of three injections, which immunises against Rabies.

MENANGLE

Another new virus called Menangle virus recently infected animals in a piggery near Sydney, causing sows to abort their unborn young. The virus also infected several people working in the piggery, causing symptoms similar to severe influenza. Flying foxes from a nearby colony were tested and found to have antibodies for the Menangle virus. Further testing revealed that flying foxes in Far North Queensland also carried antibodies to Menangle virus. Whether flying foxes carry the virus and are the primary source of the virus has not been established.

Why these viruses have only now just appeared, why and how flying foxes are involved in their transmission, and how long these viruses have been in Australia are some of the questions currently being researched by animal health authorities. There is some concern that the increased contact or the close proximity of wildlife to domestic animals has had an important role in their emergence. It is known that wildlife species carry many viruses which are benign to that particular species, but when one of these viruses crosses over to a new species, particularly a domestic animal, it becomes lethal. With the increasing loss of their natural habitat and the provision of a more reliable food resource in suburban areas, flying foxes are being drawn into closer contact with humans and domestic animals. On the positive side, due to the ease in locating their camps, and the similarities in their physiology to humans, flying foxes are becoming important sentinels for monitoring the health of our community.

BEHAVIOUR

Much of the behaviour related to flight, mating, birthing and raising young has been discussed in earlier chapters. The following refers to more general modes of behaviour, both of individual bats and in camps. Feeding is covered in Chapter 8, and mass movements and migrations in Chapter 9.

NOCTURNAL BEHAVIOUR

Unlike some Pacific Island flying foxes, Australian flying foxes forage almost exclusively during the night. Flying foxes leave their camps at dusk, sometimes just before sundown or shortly after dark. The departure time appears to be influenced by food availability. If food is in short supply, or a long distance from the camp, flying foxes will leave the camp before sundown. When food is relatively abundant, or located nearby, or during periods of a full moon, flying foxes will leave camp well after dark.

Flying foxes on the wing during the day — because of a disturbance or during food shortages (see below) — may be attacked by a range of avian species. Flying foxes have been seen being harassed by Willie wagtails (*Rhipidura leucophrys*), butcher birds (*Craticus torquatus*, *C. nigrogularis*), pied currawongs (*Strepera graculina*),

Torresian crows (*Corvus orru*), Brahminy kites (*Haliastur indus*), and white-breasted sea-eagles (*Haliaeetus leucogaster*). Only the last two species can be regarded as serious predators.

The exodus from a camp usually consists of streams of bats heading off in the direction of the food source. Some of these favoured pathways utilise rivers and saddles in ridges to the point where they are permanent exits from the camps. Other routes change as food sources appear and disappear.

Circling and wheeling in the camp prior to the exodus may be related to information transfer, or just warming up. When the first animal decides to leave the camp in a particular direction, others follow. Sometimes the leader then turns around and flies back and joins the resulting column. This may happen several times until the front of the column is spread out and becomes dispersed.

Again, depending on the quality of food and its distance from the camp, flying foxes commence to return at all stages of the night. The peak of returns occurs just before dawn, and bats can be seen returning along the familiar pathways used in their exodus at the beginning of the night.

Despite most people being aware of flying foxes feeding in trees at night, there have been very few documented reports on feeding behaviour. What is known is discussed in Chapter 8.

CAMPS AND ROOSTING BEHAVIOUR

CAMP LOCATION

In most cases, flying foxes establish their camps in tall and reasonably dense vegetation. Camps sites that are used for extensive periods must allow for a certain amount of movement within the camp site for roosting flying foxes. This allows vegetation, damaged as a result of flying-fox roosting activities, to recover. Continual usage, or dense numbers of roosting flying foxes, can severely damage vegetation, sometimes killing trees or stripping them bare of leaves.

Little red flying foxes cause the most destruction of vegetation at camp sites. Their habit of forming dense clusters, with up to 30 bats hanging together from one small branch, often results in the branch breaking (see Plate 14). The combined weight of many such clusters will cause even large branches to break under the total body weight. The resulting effect of a camp of little reds on a patch of vegetation is somewhat akin to the damage done by a severe hail or wind storm.

Fortunately these large camps of little reds are mobile, and move on when the local flowering ceases. This is usually after a four- to six-week stay, and they may or may not return to the same camp site the next year. This allows the camp-site vegetation to recover. However, as the choices of camp site get more restricted due to forest clearing, particularly in eastern Australia, secure sites are being visited more often, and the damaged vegetation does not get a chance to recover. These camps are frequently the urban sites, and ones that are already occupied by black or grey-headed flying foxes.

There are also many instances of flying foxes setting up camps in suburban areas, often when there appears to be plenty of alternate and suitable habitat available elsewhere. There are obvious advantages in establishing camps near humans: they are safer from shooting parties; there are more reliable food resources from regularly watered suburban trees; and street lights are possibly used at night as a navigational aid. With the increase of urban sprawl, flying fox camps that were once located in rural settings are now on the edge of suburbia. Many old camp sites have been lost due to development, or abandoned because of continuous disturbance or a lack of reliable food.

There are some local exceptions to the general camp location observed of individual species. At Chillagoe, north Queensland, and in Tunnel Creek Cave in the Kimberley area of Western Australia, black flying foxes roost in dolines, or the open collapsed areas of caves in limestone outcrops. There is evidence at Chillagoe that a number of

Figure 7.1
A section of this camp of black flying foxes on Cliff Island, Cape York, has been disturbed and the flying foxes are moving away from human visitors. They are keeping close to and in the canopy of mangroves due to the presence of a white-bellied sea eagle patrolling the sky immediately above the camp.
(Les Hall)

these cave-type roost sites are regularly used and this is probably a result of these areas having a favourable, protected microclimate, while the surrounding country has a lack of suitable vegetation. Occasionally some camps are located in lower vegetation, such as in the mangroves at Auckland Creek at Gladstone. Here, the mangroves are only 1–3 metres tall, but the area is surrounded by water and protected from wind by earthen banks.

Black and grey-headed flying foxes camps have also been observed located close to, or beside a creek or river. Camp sites are also found in swampy areas. Locations on creeks and rivers would have obvious advantages for ease of navigation when returning to camp during the night. Location beside rivers or creeks, or over swampy areas, also make access to the camp by ground-based predators more difficult.

BEHAVIOUR IN CAMP

Despite their living in communal camps being one of the most characteristic features of flying foxes, very little is known about their formation and social composition. Camps can be classified into a number of broad categories. Some camps are more or less permanent, although the numbers of bats occupying them may vary during the year, and the camp may be vacated for several weeks during local food shortages. Other camps are regarded as seasonal, and usually fulfil social as well as feeding requirements.

Summer camps, which are used from September to March, are usually the largest. During this time young are born and raised, territories are established and defended, the selection of mates for the next breeding cycle is made, and conception occurs. These camps are particularly noisy and there is constant activity throughout the day.

For the rest of the year camps are smaller and quieter and their presence is determined by local food availability. The period from mid-April to early September is the quietest time in the camp. It is also the time when camps break up and move, and transient animals will use temporary, or join established, camps. Large camps often become fragmented and smaller bivouac camps can be established during periods of local food abundance. These small camps usually only last a week or so, and often contain segregated sexes and age classes. It is during this period that major population shifts occur.

Juveniles still associate in large groups, and during the day bicker among themselves. Aggressive behaviour involving three or four young — with lots of biting and wing flapping — occurs, but is quickly broken up by adult bats who scatter the young.

Bare-backed flying foxes have been observed roosting in a massive boulder pile at the mouth of the Pascoe River on Cape York. Other roosts have been found under rocky overhangs covered with vegetation, and even in an old abandoned mine. The roost sites of this

Figure 7.2
Bare-backed flying foxes roost in a complex maze of passageways in this pile of huge boulders near the mouth of the Pascoe River on Cape York. Note the size of humans on the beach in the foreground. (Les Hall)

species have some characteristic features. All sites where this bat has been found are in partial darkness in the daytime. Another of the obvious features of the camps is the spacing of the bats. There appears to be no obvious reason why the bats could not hang from anywhere under the rocks, yet they roost mostly in small groups. Stains from the skin glands on the bats mark the underside surface of the boulders where they roost.

Not much is known about their social behaviour. Reports from people visiting the camp on the Pascoe River vary in the estimate of the numbers present. Locating all the groups of bare-backed flying foxes in the boulder pile without them mixing is difficult and there are numerous passageways and exits for the bats to escape. The largest estimates of group size are of several hundred, and the smallest 50–60 bats. This variation in numbers could reflect seasonal movements, or the presence of an alternative roost site.

RESTING, MOVING AND TAKING OFF

Flying foxes hang upside-down in trees in their camp site. Normally they suspend themselves by both feet, but may also hang by one leg only. When this is the case the leg not in use is folded down and forward and covered by the wing membrane, or it can be dangled loose in hot weather. While roosting, the wings are folded beside the body.

When sleeping or during cold or rainy weather, they are wrapped around the body forming a membranous coat. In hot weather a wing is dropped and fanned to cool circulating blood (see pages 24–25).

Slow movements are made along a perch in a shuffling bipedal manner. Faster movement along a perch or when climbing is performed in a quadrupedal fashion, with the two thumbs used as hooks, and the wing membranes folded tightly. Flying foxes appear to be ambidextrous. Vertical trunks of trees are climbed quadrupedally with the head uppermost.

Landings in branches are usually performed with precision where the bat passes over the limb and grips it with its trailing feet and then swings down to an upside-down position. At other times landings can be an uncontrolled crash into vegetation. This usually occurs with unfamiliarity of the roost, or by juveniles learning to fly.

Defecation and urination are performed by the bats inverting themselves and hanging by their thumbs. After the job is completed, they give a deft pelvic shake and return to their upside-down position (Plate 19).

To become airborne, flying foxes flap rapidly with both wings until their body is almost horizontal, which unlocks the tendons which hold the toes at right-angles while roosting (see 'Feet', page 28). Flying foxes can take off from flat ground by pushing down with their forearms. If a flying fox accidentally lands in water, it cannot take off from the surface. They are good swimmers, however, and will swim to the bank or to a tree in the water, and climb until sufficient height is gained for takeoff.

SOCIAL BEHAVIOUR

GROOMING

A considerable amount of a flying fox's non-flying time is spent grooming its fur. This is done mainly with the claws of the hind feet in a scratching manner. The thumb claw is also used, and occasionally biting of fur is seen.

The wings and genitals are licked and the muzzle area is pushed into the wing membrane, no doubt transferring sebum from the abundant glands associated with the hair follicles on the muzzle. This behaviour may also rupture the small lipid droplets produced in the wing membrane epidermis and help waterproof the wings.

Licking of the ano-genital area is a prominent adult male activity, particularly during the breeding season. Females may reciprocate, especially just prior to copulation. Females lick their young immediately after birth and for several months afterwards. Urination on the fur followed by licking occurs in males at anytime during the year, but most frequently during the mating season.

VOCALISATION

Flying foxes are very vocal animals, and are probably the next most vocal group of mammals after primates and cetaceans. Studies on their acoustic behaviour show that their calls are in the range of 4–6 kHz. This is closely matched by their hearing ability (see 'Ears and hearing', page 38), which is similar in range to humans. This is one reason why we have the anthropomorphic attitude that flying foxes are 'noisy' animals.

Vocalisations play an important role in the social behaviour of flying foxes. Over thirty different types of calls have been recorded for grey-headed flying foxes. These calls include mother/young, male/female, male/male and female/female calls which are associated with specific behaviour patterns. Adult males have distinctive local calls in the mating season, and the call of juveniles is a high pitched squeak. The noises made by squabbling flying foxes in their food trees attracts other flying foxes. These noisy territorial disputes are an integral part of the 'residents and raiders' model of feeding (see page 81).

FRUIT BATS AND BLOSSOM BATS

It is very difficult to locate tube-nosed fruit bats, as they are solitary and very well camouflaged in the sub-canopy layer of dense vegetation where they roost. Consequently very few observations have been made on their behaviour.

Tube-nosed fruit bats are found in rainforest, riparian forest, or dense wet sclerophyll. They usually fly along tracks in the forest 3–5 metres above the ground, but will fly much higher if feeding on emergent fig trees. In most cases these bats may be caught in mistnets set at night along tracks or over creeks in dense vegetation with a closed canopy. Because they have a recognisable eye-shine and a distinctive high-pitched whistle, these bats can also be surveyed at night using a spotlight. Finding them during the day is very difficult as their spotted wings and brown colour make them look like dead leaves. They have been found hanging in or near similarly sized dead leaves around two metres above the ground, and not far off a track in closed forest. The roost site is never far from the food source and the bat will roost in the same location day after day while the food source remains.

When feeding, a number of individuals will often congregate around the same fruiting tree. In these situations, bats will fly up to the tree, bite off a ripe fruit, and then fly some distance away and eat it. The fruit is carried in the mouth while flying, but when the bat arrives at its perch, it forms a sling by hanging on to the perch by its feet and thumbs. It then places the fruit on its chest and commences to bite pieces off. Using this technique, the bat hides the fruit from the view of other fruit bats, and has a reasonably flat surface where it can manipulate the fruit.

Tube-nosed fruit bats are often particularly aggressive towards one another and it is difficult to keep more than one in a cage. Most disputes are caused by competition for food, but these bats do seem to like being completely solitary. A single high-pitched whistle of a constant frequency is often emitted while flying, but the function of the call is not known.

It was once thought that the function of the elongated tubular nostrils in tube-nosed fruit bats was to allow it to breath while its face was immersed in mushy fruit. The nostrils are well separated and have internal musculature which allows them to change the width or diameter of each nostril independently, as well as the direction in which it points. Recent observations have shown that this bat is in fact a tidy eater. Their tubular nostrils do not appear to get in the way while they are eating and are more than likely used for the directional location of food, which in most areas is figs.

Both species of blossom bat are solitary and roost in the subcanopy of dense vegetation where they too resemble hanging dead leaves. No groups or colonies have ever been found, but like tube-nosed fruit bats, numbers of blossom bats will congregate around an isolated food tree. Although separate visits to flowers by individuals can be very brief, blossom bats show a high fidelity to their feeding areas and will vigorously defend them from other individuals by attacking, vocalising, and clapping the tips of their wings together. Short chases around food trees have been observed.

Movements seem to be dictated by the availability of food and roost sites. They generally roost close to their food supply and move on when the food diminishes. blossom bats will commute from as little as 50 metres to at least 6 kilometres from their roost in rainforest areas to a heathland feeding site. In the southern part of its range, the Queensland blossom bat feeds in the coastal heaths at night and returns to the shelter of rainforest vegetation, where the microclimate is moist, to roost during the day. Roost departure in the evening is dependent on levels of light, and will vary with the moon phase and distance to food. During a full moon, blossom bats delay their departure from the roost for up to 4 hours. On nights following the full moon, departure times are 5–20 minutes after dark.

Marking and observing individuals shows that male Queensland blossom bats are more likely than females to be faithful to a site (in this case of *Banksia integrifolia*) during the flowering season. This suggests that females are more mobile and probably seek out the areas with highest nectar production, while most males stay put, probably after they have established feeding territories. Their aggressive behaviour and fidelity to one site, plus observations of their reactions to intruder pressure, support the idea that these bats are territorial and indicate that much is yet to be learnt about their interesting social systems.

DIET AND FEEDING ECOLOGY

DIGESTIVE SYSTEM

The palate of all megachiropterans is deeply ridged. The tongue is used to crush and pulp food against it. The bare-backed flying fox has prominent cheek pouches, which it undoubtedly uses to carry fruit. The tongue of flying foxes is covered with small pointed papillae, the arrangement of which is different for each species and reflects their different food preferences (Figure 8.1). Taste buds are located on the tip of the tongue of grey-headed and black flying foxes, while they are only found at the base of the tongue in little reds. This suggests that the former two species sample and test their food when feeding, while little reds are more obligate feeders and feed on one type of food.

The tongues of tube-nosed fruit bats are covered with flattened papillae (protrusions) which allow it to handle hard-skinned fruit. This contrasts with the delicate brush-like papillae found on the tongue of the nectariferous blossom bats, which are similar in appearance to those found in lorikeets and honeyeaters. There are four large circumvalate papillae on the tongue of tube-nosed bats, where all other bats have three or less. The inner lips of tube-nosed bats are also densely fringed with small papillae which probably help to hold fruit in the mouth.

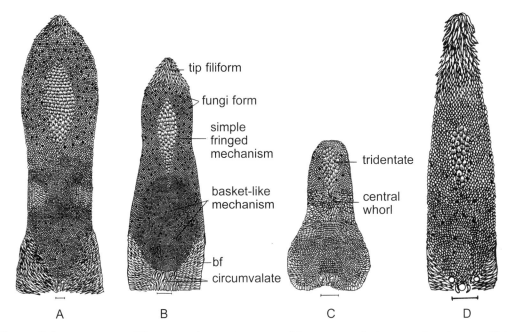

A   B   C   D

Figure 8.1
Patterns in the papillae on the dorsal surface of megachiropterans' tongues are distinctive to each species, and reflect their food type. The widened tip of the grey headed's tongue (A) helps extract juice and manipulate fruit in the mouth; the tapered tongue of the little red flying fox (B) is used to probe flowers for nectar. The tongue of the eastern tubenosed fruit bat (C), a fruit specialist, is club-like with few types of papillae. The long filamentous papillae on the tip of the tongue of the Queensland blossom bat (D) are used to extract flower nectar. (Drawings by Patrina Birt)

The oesophagus in megachiropterans is long and quite small in diameter, and leads to a simple saccular stomach which is usually empty. As discussed below, food transit time through the gut of flying foxes is extremely fast and most of the digestive process for the evening's food is completed by early next morning, leaving the stomach empty for most of the day. This appears to be true for tube-nosed and blossom bats also. The cardiac region of the stomach of tube-nosed and blossom bats appears as a conical enlargement of the oesophagus and is lined with stratified squamous epithelium. The liver consists of three lobes which wrap around the stomach.

Although the stomach has distinct cardiac and fundic regions, there is no obvious separation between the small and large intestine in flying foxes, and there is no caecum or appendix. The gastrointestinal tracts of grey-headed and black flying foxes have well developed villi (folds), covered with absorptive cells which have relatively long microvilli, which increases their absorptive surface area. The large intestine, although relatively short, is highly folded, thereby increasing its surface area.

These anatomical features allow flying foxes to process large quantities of food quite rapidly. Food transit times range from 12–34 minutes. In contrast, pollen, which is ingested with nectar, takes 50 (*Callistemon*) to 163 (*Banksia*) minutes to appear in the faeces of the Queensland blossom bat. The gut passage rates for pollen in blossom bats are, however, considerably faster than the passage rates of other pollen-feeding animals.

Fruit-eating bats can ingest up to two-and-a-half times their body-weight in plant products each night. By manipulating the energy and protein content of a captive individual's diet, it has been shown that fruit intake is determined by the protein content of the fruit exploited. Fruit-eating bats appear to be obliged to over-ingest energy to obtain sufficient protein, which would explain the requirement for an efficient digestive tract. This suggests that the rapid transit time of food allows fruit-eating bats to reduce the bulk of food carried in flight, consequently reducing the energy expenditure associated with foraging. The field energy budget of the grey-headed flying fox is 944 kilojoules per kilogram-0.75_d^{-1}: suggesting that the low basal metabolic rate of this bat is associated with an interrupted or restricted source of dietary nitrogen.

DIET

Details of the diet of Australian flying foxes have been extensively observed and studied, and may form one of the better known aspects of their ecology. A list of plant species known to be consumed by flying-foxes is given in the Appendix. The list includes all plant parts consumed by flying foxes, including fruit, nectar, pollen, stamens and flower parts, leaves and bark.

The larger body size of flying foxes generally restricts their access to food to the outer canopy, so they tend to range long distances and depend on less plant species as a food resource. In the northern rainforests, the bare-backed flying fox avoids this problem by having added manoeuvrability as a result of its extended wing surface area, and can fly and feed below the canopy as well. This allows the bare-backed flying fox access to a greater variety of food types. The smaller body size and wing shape of tube-nosed and blossom bats also allows them to utilise a wide range of plant species for food, and consequently results in them having much smaller home ranges than flying foxes.

Flying foxes show a variety of characteristics that suggest differing ecological roles. Spectacled flying foxes have a specialist association with rainforest, whereas other species such as little red flying foxes specialise upon blossom and nectar. The size and shape of the molariform dentition of flying foxes can give an indication to the degree of mastication necessary in their feeding. Those species having a nectarivorous diet possess molars which are reduced in size: frugivorous species have heavier dentition.

On the basis of dental characters and known diet, it is possible to allocate Australian flying foxes to broad categories that reflect their general ecology. Specialists species are considered to be those estimated to have approximately 90 per cent of their food as one type, generalists have a broader diet.

Figure 8.2
Moreton Bay figs
(*Ficus macrophylla*)
are eaten by both
black and grey-
headed flying foxes.
These figs are com-
mon in public parks
and gardens, and
flying foxes may
often be seen
around these trees
at night.

DIETARY GENERALISTS

The grey-headed flying fox has been classified as a dietary generalist, a concept supported by several studies. There is strong evidence from radio-tracking studies that colonies of this species have some individuals that primarily select blossom and others that mainly select fruit. The other dietary generalist, the black flying fox, appears to be competing with the grey-headed in the overlap of their ranges. The more adaptive black is extending its distributional limit southward, as the northern and southern limits of the grey-headed's distribution change similarly. This may be a reflection of the short evolutionary history of megachiropterans in Australia.

The diet of the bare-backed flying fox is known to include the flowers of *Eucalyptus* and *Corymbia*, flowers and fruit of rainforest trees,

and exotic fruit such as pawpaw and banana. Cluster figs and cauliflorous fruit and flowers growing on trunks and branches within the rainforest provide bare-backed flying foxes with a food source which is not generally utilised by the slightly larger black and little red flying foxes, which feed mainly on the upper outer canopy. The bare-backed flying fox has been recorded feeding on the blossoms of the northern bloodwood (*Corymbia nesophila*) adjacent to rainforest, but it is not known whether the bat's more normal food was plentiful in the rainforest at that time.

The eastern tube-nosed fruit bat is a fruit specialist, favouring figs, particularly the common and widespread cluster fig (*Ficus variegata*). Other figs (*F. copiosa* and *F. nodosa*), as well as the blue quandong (*Eleaocarpus grandis*), Burdekin plum (*Pleiogyniun timorense*) and other fleshy fruit are also eaten. Unfortunately this bat has acquired a taste for introduced guavas (*Psidium guajava*) on which it feeds and whose seeds it spreads.

Observations on the feeding behaviour of eastern fruit bats around a cluster fig show that the bats frequently fly up to the fig tree, bite off a ripe fruit and then carry the fruit away for up to 50 metres, where it perches and consumes the fruit. Figs weighing up to 15 grams can be carried by tube-nosed bats. This behaviour is particularly noticeable when there are a number of tube-nosed bats feeding at one tree, and is similar to the 'raiders and residents' model seen in flying-fox feeding behaviour (see page 81). It is an important mechanism for the dispersal of the seeds away from the parent plant.

Figure 8.3
The strong jaw muscles and dentition of tube-nosed fruit bats allows them to feed on the fruit of *Randia sessilis* from north Queensland. The fruit of this tree has an extremely hard outer coat which is difficult to penetrate, even by a human with a knife. *Top*: Intact fruit; *Bottom*: Fruit which has been opened and eaten by tube-nosed fruit bats. (Greg Richards)

While both blossom bat species are regarded as blossom specialists, there appears to be some variation in the involvement of fruit and leaf material in their diet. In the southern parts of the Queensland blossom bat's range it appears to be mainly a nectarivore, while in north-east Queensland they are facultative frugivores and, to a lesser extent folivores. Fig seeds, particularly from the female fruit of a number of figs (*Ficus varigata*, *F. congesta*, and *F. racemosa*) and seeds of *Timonius* are frequently found in their faeces. Only a small amount of fruit remains has been found in their droppings in northern New South Wales. This variation in diet could be the result of competition between the two blossom bats, or differences in availability of fruit and nectar. When blossom bats visit flowers and feed on nectar, pollen is collected by the special scale-like projections on the fur of Queensland blossom bats. Pollen is ingested while feeding and when the bat grooms itself, and is an important source of nitrogen in its diet. The pollen is also transferred from one plant to the next via the body fur of the bat.

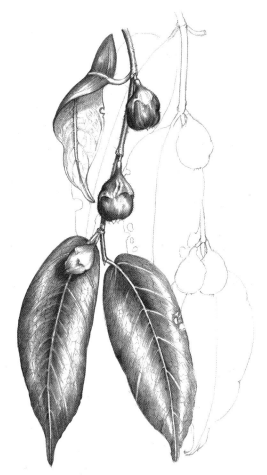

Figure 8.4
The sandpaper fig (*Ficus coronata*) is part of the diet of the eastern tube-nosed fruit bat.

In tropical Australia, the Queensland blossom bat feeds on nectar and pollen of a variety of rainforest trees, including the cauliflorous *Syzygium*, and will visit orchards where durian (*Durio zibethinus*) and wax jambu (*S. jambos*) are flowering. In a study of the pollination of the rainforest tree *S. cormiflorum* it was shown that blossom bats were the single most important pollinators, in spite of a far greater activity of birds and insects in the tree. The floral biology of *S. cormiflorum* is regarded as that of a chiropterophilous plant — as it produces copious amounts of weak nectar.

In the southern limits of its range, heathland and *Melaleuca* swamps are critical feeding habitats for the Queensland blossom bat. In these areas *Banksia*, *Melaleuca* and *Callistemon* and certain eucalypts (such as the swamp mahogany, *Eucalyptus robusta*) are favoured sources of food. Subtropical rainforest and coastal eucalypt forest are visited when heaths and paperbarks are not flowering. The ability to disperse seeds, and the pollen-carrying capacity of their fur, points to the importance of blossom bats in the maintenance of their habitat.

Figure 8.5
The cauliflorous flowers of this *Syzygium cormiflorum* attract a large number of nectar-seeking insects, birds and mammals. The Queensland blossom bat has been shown to be the most effective pollinator of this important rainforest tree. (Greg Richards)

FRUIT DIETS

The spectacled flying fox is the largest frugivorous specialist pteropodid in Australia and has the most restricted distribution of the four species found on the mainland. It is found only in coastal north-eastern Queensland, and shows a close association with tracts of rainforest, roosting either within it or not further than 7 kilometres away. Data on the foods eaten by the spectacled flying fox obtained over a five-year period recorded the fruits of 26 native trees, all of which were rainforest canopy species. The flowers of ten tree species were also eaten, three of which were found in rainforest, the remainder being sclerophyll forest members.

It has been suggested that the colour and form of presentation of fruit may be a pattern that influences choice by fruit-eating bats. Of a small sample of natural fruits in the diet of the spectacled flying fox, it was found that 22 out of 25 were in light-coloured categories, and the majority were presented on the periphery (outer branches) of the tree canopy.

Using a paint colour chart and low-light photography, the colours of fruits eaten were recorded and ranked according to their visibility. The majority of diet fruits were in the category of highest visibility (at night), as shown in Table 8.1. The significant relationship between the visibility of particular colours at low light levels and the colours of fruits selected by the spectacled flying fox indicated that visual cues played an important role in food location. The highly developed areas in the brain controlling vision and olfaction in flying foxes (see Brain, nervous system and senses, page 33, and Eyes and vision, page 36) confirms the importance of colour and smell in selecting food.

TABLE 8.1 FRUIT COLOUR GROUPS IN THE DIET OF THE SPECTACLED FLYING FOX, A SPECIALIST FRUGIVORE

Visibility group	Fruit colours	Number of natural fruits	Number of cultivated fruits	Total fruits
3	white cream light pink yellow	13	5	18
2	orange lilac light blue light green	9	8	17
1	red	1	0	1
0	purple*	2	0	2
Totals		25	13	38

*beachfront vegetation

Note: Colours were allocated a visibility ranking by a photographic method: Group 1 colours were visible only at a light level approximating moonlight; Group 2 colours were visible under normal light levels; Group 3 colours were visible at lower light levels; Group 0 colours were not visible even in dim light.

Source: After Richards 1990b.

Spectacled flying foxes feed primarily in rainforest, though they are also known to feed on purple-coloured fruits such as beach almonds (*Terminalia* spp.) along the ocean shore. Presumably the location of the trees plays an important role in food location in this case. The fruit trees' favouring of flying foxes by providing light-coloured fruit leads to the theory that many tree species are likely to be solely dependent upon megachiropterans for seed dispersal, especially since red-coloured fruits which are hard to see at night are usually consumed by fruit-eating birds such as rainforest pigeons during the day. (See Hypothesis of co-dependence, page 81.)

Fruits utilised by grey-headed and black flying foxes in north-eastern New South Wales have a high pulp water content (averaging 80 per cent by weight), are relatively sweet (averaging 15 per cent sucrose equivalents), and are presented in dense clumps. Unlike the fruit specialist spectacled flying fox, the dietary generalist grey-headed flying fox does not use colour to select fruit.

It is obvious why mangoes (*Mangifera indica*) are so attractive to flying foxes. The ripe fruit is pale coloured, highly aromatic and is located on the outer branches of the tree: all features which attract flying foxes. This suggests that mangoes have had a long relationship with flying foxes, well before the fruit was ever introduced to Australia. In its original natural distribution of India and South-East Asia, mangoes are mainly dependent on flying foxes for seed dispersal.

Of the other fruit-eating species, the bare-backed flying fox, which inhabits the wet tropical forests, feeds on fruiting trees such as lillypillies and figs. It is also known to feed in the drier forests on both fruit and flowers. Tube-nosed fruit bats are fig specialists. Numerous species of figs are found throughout the distribution of tube-nosed bats. Figs are known to have asynchronous fruiting (each tree fruits at a different time), which provides a year-round food resource.

FLOWER DIETS

The major proportion of the flower diet of megachiropterans in Australia comes from the Family Myrtaceae, and in particular the genera *Eucalyptus*, *Corymbia*, *Melaleuca*, *Angophora* and *Syncarpia*. *Banksia* (Family Proteaceae) are also important food for flying foxes and blossom bats. These plant genera have widespread distributions in Australia's forests and woodlands. They have a geographic range that partly matches that of the megachiropterans, and are amongst the best nectar-producing genera in the northern tropics. (These tree species also support a large honey-producing industry.)

Studies of the diversity in the diet of flying foxes in the monsoonal tropics of northern Australia have revealed that the plants came from 52 species in 19 genera from 11 families, which is similar to the diversity of diet of fruit bats elsewhere in the Old World. In tropical Australia, black and little red flying foxes had similar diets, with an 85 per cent overlap in the plant species that they utilised.

Nectar is the principal food source for both blossom bat species, but while collecting nectar, they also ingest substantial amounts of pollen. The Queensland blossom bat is particularly fond of *Melaleuca* and *Banksia* in the southern parts of its distribution. In northern Australia the northern blossom bat feeds on the nectar produced by the freshwater mangrove, *Barringtonia acutangula*.

The flowers that attract and are fed on by megachiropterans have distinct characteristics. In general any flower which could be regarded as chiropterophilous, or being a 'bat flower', will possess one or more of the following features:

- location on the periphery of the tree canopy
- presence of a strong sweet or musty odour
- large inflorescence (stem bearing many flowers)
- light-coloured corolla
- contrasting flower colour against leafy background
- high numbers of anthers
- anthers which are longer than the corolla
- flowers arranged in bunches.

Figure 8.6
The flowering of the Queensland blue gum (*Eucalyptus tereticornis*) can have an important influence in flying-fox movements in south-eastern Queensland and northern New South Wales.

In a field study in northern Australia, plants visited by megachiropterans had at least five of the above characters, those not visited had fewer. Over 90 per cent of *Eucalyptus* and *Corymbia* species in south-eastern Australia show the potential to be 'bat-flowers' and could be utilised by megachiropterans. A 'honey index' has been developed to assess the potential for viable honey production of 83 eucalypt and rainforest communities on the south coast of New South Wales. Over half of these communities had a high value for honey production, and could therefore also be expected to be of value to megachiropterans.

FOLIAGE DIETS

It appears that folivory (feeding on leaves), although rarely reported, is quite widespread in flying foxes. They have been observed to feed on the leguminous *Albizia procera* and *A. lebbek*. Measurement of the liquid fraction extracted from chewed *Albizia* leaves showed about 51 per cent of the crude protein was extracted from the leaves, and was itself 36 per cent protein (on a dry-matter basis). As a nutritional strategy, the attraction of tree legume foliage for food appears to be their relatively high protein levels and lack of toxic secondary compounds. Captive flying foxes are known to eat a variety of green leaves, and even grass.

Little red flying foxes are known to tear the bark from paperbark trees (*Melaleuca* spp.). The bats appear to be eating the inner layers of bark, or the sap from these trees. After a night's feeding on one of these trees by flying foxes, the ground under the tree is strewn with bark fragments and the trunk and major limbs are covered with shredded bark.

PLANT–FLYING FOX INTERACTION

Rather than merely feeding on these plant species, it is becoming increasingly clear that megachiropterans interact as pollen vectors and seed carriers. This leads to the theory that the bats and some of the forest species are in fact co-dependant. This in turn has obvious implications for conservation considerations for both the bats and the forest communities.

POLLINATION

The early view that forest, particularly rainforest, trees were self-compatible and self-pollinated has been overturned with the current knowledge that outcrossing (being fertilised by pollen from a different tree) is a more important phenomenon. Outbreeding is the primary advantage that a plant species has in any co-dependent association with bats. Several Australian studies have identified bats as major pollen vectors, responsible for the movement of genetic material from one tree to another.

Most woody plants in Australian forests, especially members of the families Myrtaceae and Proteaceae, are obligate outbreeders. Gene flow is particularly important in the genera *Eucalyptus* and *Corymbia*, which is characterised by high levels of outcrossing, and reduced viability in seeds from self-pollinated flowers.

Radio-collared grey-headed flying foxes feeding on *Melaleuca quinquenervia* and blossoms of various *Eucalyptus* and *Corymbia* were shown to be highly mobile, feeding through the night on several trees within a stand as well as moving between stands of the same flowering species that were several kilometres apart. The grey-headed flying fox is therefore a potentially efficient pollen vector.

Thousands of viable pollen grains were collected each night on the body fur of foraging black and little red flying foxes during a study in the Northern Territory. Movements of animals from plant to plant indicated that more pollen is moved a greater distance by bats than other vertebrate flower visitors. Most tree species in the diet of megachiropterans grow in multi-species communities and it is rare in these communities that two conspecific trees grow side-by-side. Pollinators of any species must therefore regularly move 50 metres or more to transport pollen to the nearest flowering conspecific.

Observations on little red flying foxes showed that only 5 per cent of movements from flowering tree to flowering tree were 10 metres or less. In the movements of nectarivorous birds, such as honeyeaters, 80 per cent of movements between flowering plants are in the order of 10 metres and only occasionally as long as 50–100 metres. Although not shown with experimental rigidity, this evidence suggests strongly that megachiropterans are the most likely (or only) vectors of outcrossed pollen in eucalypt forests and woodlands.

Although it is highly likely that bats have the potential to be a major pollinator in eucalypt-dominated ecosystems, the question remains as to whether the pollen transported is viable. It has been shown that 78 per cent of pollen grains removed from black and little red flying foxes in the Northern Territory were of high enough quality to ensure fertilisation. (Viable grains were considered to be those that were full and had the intine layer unbroken: non-viable grains were those that had their contents evacuated.) Other researchers have observed that although the number of grains was high, the majority of the pollen from the heads of bats was damaged (ruptured by grooming with saliva) and they were useless for fertilisation. However, most grains collected on the back and chest of each animal were intact. On average, only 60 per cent of grains on the head of a foraging bat were viable, compared with 87 per cent on the chest, and 77 per cent on the back of the body. It has been shown that megachiropterans carry significantly greater pollen loads than those published for other bats, and greater than all other Australian flower-visiting vertebrates. The ability of flying foxes to carry larger pollen loads than other vertebrates is most likely attributable to their larger body size, being at least ten times that of honeyeaters.

Having established that flying foxes are efficient pollen vectors, the proof that do they actually transfer pollen and cause fertilisation to occur also needed experimental testing. This was done by covering flower buds of *Eucalyptus porrecta* and *E. confertiflora* in a northern Australian study area, to prevent contamination with unspecified pollen. Tagged and covered buds were rubbed with the head of a live flying fox when the buds flowered (568 flowers on 16 trees), and buds were recovered. Fruit set, only possible through the agency of the 'experimental' flying fox, was later observed. Thus megachiropterans can facilitate fertilisation.

Current studies on nectar production in commercially important hardwood eucalypts in south-east Queensland by Patrina Birt have shown that the majority of nectar is produced by these trees at night. The nectar fed on by lorikeets, honeyeaters and bees during the day is the left-over from the previous night's flow. In addition, the production and release of pollen is greatest at night, and flowers are more receptive to fertilisation during the night. Although eucalypts can self-pollinate, it is obvious that they have evolved to attract a nocturnal pollinator. Some moths could play a role, but it appears that flying foxes have the major role in pollination and pollen distribution in these hardwood forests. This research is continuing.

Overall, there is a great deal of evidence that megachiropterans, and particularly flying foxes, play a vital pollination role in forest ecosystems in Australia.

SEED DISPERSAL

Wide-ranging seed dispersal encourages genetic exchange between fragments of forest or isolated populations of particular species, decreasing the amount of genetic subdivision of taxa. Since the success of self-regeneration for many tropical trees improves if their propagules are moved away from the parent tree, those tree species that encourage visitation by flying foxes ensure that such a process occurs.

In Australia, flying foxes and tube-nosed fruit bats may be the only seed dispersal agent for many rainforest trees, and therefore play an important role in the long-term survival of some tree species. Furthermore, it appears that these species, whose fruit is dispersed only by flying foxes, may be 'pivotal' species. Although most species of trees produce when other fruits are readily available in the forest, these pivotal species bear fruit during periods of scarcity of other fruit, and consequently supply food for fruit-eating birds and mammals which are critical for the dispersal and ultimate recruitment of many tree species at other times of the year.

Rainforest pigeons in the wet tropics prefer to feed upon fruits that are brightly coloured (red and purple), exactly the opposite colours to those selected by spectacled flying foxes (white and yellow: see Table 8.1, page 75). This suggests that within Australian rainforest ecosystems, where flying foxes and fruit pigeons are sympatric, rainforest canopy tree communities may share the suite of dispersal agents that are available.

Data on which species' seeds are dispersed by spectacled flying foxes was obtained by identifying seedlings raised from their droppings. The source of these seeds was from faecal material collected under day roosts in the forest, and the seeds were germinated in a glasshouse with a rainforest microclimate. Twenty-six species of rainforest trees, predominantly those bearing pale-coloured fruit, were identified. Many of the tree species are those which bear fruit on their outer branches. Spectacled flying foxes have an oesophageal lumen, distendable to 4–5 millimetres, which places a limit to the size of seeds that it can transported internally. However, these small seeds could be dispersed up to 20 kilometres.

Germination trials of both ingested and ejected seeds from grey-headed flying foxes in New South Wales showed that all but one of the plant species incorporated in the diet were viable after dispersal by these bats.

Local movements during the night determine the extent to which seeds may be dispersed. Radio-tracking has shown that direct line distances from roosts to initial feeding trees ranged from 4–32 kilometres, and on any night individual animals visited a number of feeding trees located several kilometres apart.

THE 'RESIDENTS AND RAIDERS' MODEL

During observations made on the behaviour of groups of spectacled flying foxes when feeding at night, it became apparent that individuals defended a 'feeding territory', the size of which appeared to be spatially constrained rather than being related to food density, and was 3 metres or so in diameter. These territories were actively defended, but particularly so when other spectacled flying foxes that had fed elsewhere attempted to join the feeding group. This 'raid' resulted in vocalisation and threats from a territory 'resident' immediately after the new bat landed. The 'raider' was chased from one territory to another by other residents whose boundaries were crossed, the result being the eviction of the 'raider' from the tree (Figure 8.7, page 83). On many occasions these raiders carried fruit from the last feeding territory as they were being evicted. Raiders were apparently unable to carry large fruit with large seeds for long distances, eventually dropping them within 100 metres or so from the source trees, hence dispersing the seed at a distance from the parent.

This is important, as it has been shown that seedlings growing at a distance from the parent tree have a greater chance of survival to maturity than those growing closer the parent. The 'raiders versus residents' behaviour leads to the assumption that spectacled flying foxes have an integral role in seed dispersal and the regeneration of a suite of rainforest trees, particularly those having light-coloured fruit, and this is further influenced by the density of the flying-fox population.

HYPOTHESIS OF CO-DEPENDENCE

Megachiropterans have shared a long association with angiosperms (flowering plants). These plants probably evolved in the South-East Asian region around 130 million years ago and achieved world-wide dominance over the gymnosperms (conifers) about 90 million years ago. The first recognisable rainforest formations were in existence 60 million years ago, and the oldest megachiropteran fossils are roughly 35 million years old. It appears that frugivory in megachiropterans arose before nectarivory. Although it would stand to reason that, given the long period of co-evolution, a strong association between bats and plants would exist, a review of evidence is necessary before this conclusion can be fully appreciated.

The evidence in support of the concept of a co-dependent relationship between forest trees and megachiropterans includes:

- flying foxes have large olfactory bulbs, and olfaction is important in food location
- the eyes of Megachiroptera are highly adapted for nocturnal vision, being particularly suited to recognising light colours
- the distribution patterns of flying foxes and myrtaceous forest are closely correlated
- given normal conditions (without droughts), and given the migratory abilities of flying foxes, myrtaceous forests and woodlands provide a constant food supply throughout the year for these animals
- all ecological niches in forest in Australia available to megachiropterans are filled by at least one common specialist and several less abundant specialists
- *Eucalyptus* flowers have most of the characteristics that indicate bat pollination syndrome: particularly odour and colour
- flying foxes have been shown to be competent pollen vectors, a large proportion (over 70 per cent) of pollen is carried undamaged, and as vectors they satisfy the requirements of the

Figure 8.7
The 'raiders and residents' model. Resident spectacled flying foxes (A) protect an area in a food tree from raiding bats (B). The raiders are forced to grab a mouthful of food and eventually retreat to another tree, thus ensuring that fruit and seeds from the fruiting tree are carried away. With some tree species, the seeds from fruit dropped by resident bats will not germinate under the parent tree. Fallen fruit relies on other animals (which may include others such as cassowary) to disperse it away from the parent, or it is consumed or decomposes under the tree.

Myrtaceae for outcrossing (requirements less satisfied by other vertebrates)

- pollen transferred by flying foxes will cause fertilisation to occur
- the syndrome of mass flowering by many Myrtaceae, which draws large populations of flying foxes as pollen vectors from long distances, supports the concept that a mutually advantageous system between bats and plants exists
- Myrtaceae blossom is the primary food for blossom-eating flying foxes and blossom bats
- most of the fruits known to be eaten by flying foxes fit the bat-plant syndrome, particularly their light colour and presentation on the periphery of the tree
- germination trials of both ingested and ejected seeds of approximately 60 species showed that all but one was viable after dispersal by flying foxes
- flying foxes and tube-nosed fruit bats may be the only seed dispersal agent in Australia for many rainforest trees, and therefore play an important role in the long-term survival of some taxa
- feeding territoriality (the 'raiders versus residents' model), gives further support to the notion that a mutually advantageous system between bats and plants exists.

The evidence that a mutually advantageous system is in existence for all flying foxes appears to be overwhelming. In most situations where bat species have been well studied, co-dependence can also be shown. Myrtaceae appear to be highly dependent upon flying foxes in Australia for outcrossed pollination, and a large suite of rainforest tree species are dependent upon them for pollination and seed dispersal, yet without these food sources this family of bats would not exist.

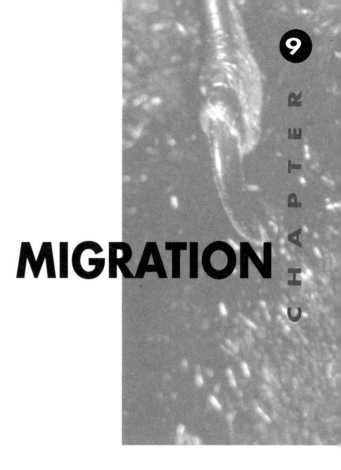

CHAPTER 9

MIGRATION

Several studies have shown that the movement patterns of flying foxes are related to the local availability of food: a decline in food supply causes migration from one area to another with an abundant food source. This occurs for both frugivorous and nectarivorous species, and even dietary generalists, although in different ways.

BROAD-SCALE MIGRATIONS: INFLUENCE OF FOOD AVAILABILITY

There is little information on the availability of native fruit as food for flying foxes in Australia, but nowhere are flowers or fruit in continuous supply. Observations have shown that the amount of blossom produced by any one species varies: in some years most of the trees of a species in an area flower at the same time, in other years the trees flower individually at different times over a period of 4–5 months, and in other years only a few trees may flower.

Phenological studies of fruit production in subtropical rainforests have shown a high seasonality by most species, with the greatest number of species fruiting in summer, and that winter was a period of low fruit availability. Some genera such as *Ficus* and *Solanum* have fruit throughout the year. In the rainforests of North Queensland, many tree species have a sequential fruit set and ripening related to altitude, where the fruit of coastal populations ripens earlier than in the uplands. Thus, frugivorous megachiropterans may be faced with a food supply that is highly predictable in its seasonal availability.

Although the majority of *Eucalyptus* and *Corymbia* species have extensive distributions in Australia, their flowering patterns show some seasonality and often occur sequentially along latitudinal and altitudinal gradients. In many species, individual trees or populations do not flower annually, and flowering is patchy throughout the range of some tree species. Therefore, movements of megachiropterans which feed predominantly on nectar could be expected to differ from those which are frugivorous. In fact, the highly variable availability of nectar has been shown to cause different migration patterns between different food specialists.

The intensity of flowering by Myrtaceae and Proteaceae communities has been classified to allow regional mapping of food resources, and correlated with movements and migrations of grey-headed flying foxes in New South Wales. This was based on the requirements of commercial apiarists registered with the New South Wales Department of Agriculture. Categories 1 and 2 described intensive flowering that produced sufficient nectar to obtain honey production from at least 80 beehives within a 2.25 square kilometre radius. Additionally, Category 1 flowerings produced sufficient protein from accessible pollen to support reproduction of the hive population. Category 2 flowering was not sufficient to support reproduction. Category 3 described flowering that occurred over an extensive area but was too sparse or patchy for use by apiarists. No flowering that was ranked in Categories 2 or 3 attracted any of 20 radio-tagged grey-headed flying foxes, thus only Category 1 can be assumed to be the minimal requirement as a food source for this species.

Plant species in the flower diet of megachiropterans in tropical northern Australia flower synchronously, but the month of first flowering and the period of flowering vary, hence providing a range of food throughout the year. In the monsoonal tropics of the Northern Territory, the flowering period for food trees averages 4.8 ± 1.5 months, and in tropical North Queensland it averages 3.2 ± 0.9 months. The flowering period ranged from 3–9 months in the former area, but only 2–5 months in North Queensland. Further, the North Queensland trees, which can be grouped into winter-flowering or summer-flowering species, have flowering times averaging 3.9 and 2.8 months.

Food availability for nectarivorous megachiropterans appears to be virtually continuous and therefore more reliable in the Northern Territory than in Queensland. This is reflected in the migratory patterns of flying foxes when the two regions are compared. Black and little red flying-fox camps in the Northern Territory are nearly always present and occupy sites for long periods, with only small local movements occurring. Conversely, the occupation period of 22 camp sites in northern coastal Queensland ranged from two weeks to two months. During six years of study, three large-scale migrations of little red flying fox colonies were recorded in northern Queensland. These migrations could be related to the failure of winter-flowering food trees during droughts. It is apparent that there is a correlation between the movement patterns of nectarivorous flying foxes and their food supply.

Fluctuations in rainfall also have an effect. *Eucalyptus* and *Corymbia* trees have poor flowering when rainfall is lower than normal, and may have reduced nectar production from any flowering during droughts. Excessive rain stimulates growth of leaves and branches and usually results in poor flowering. Species such as *C. maculata* that hold buds for long periods may abort them during periods of climatic stress, and other species such as *E. albens* may still flower but with reduced amounts of nectar.

MIGRATIONS BY FRUGIVOROUS SPECIES

Studies on the spectacled flying fox show that this species is a specialised frugivore, distributed only in far north-eastern Queensland, and roosting either within or adjacent to tropical rainforest. The occupancy of traditional roost sites in the Atherton-Port Douglas-Innisfail area of Queensland has been determined as either continuous or seasonal residence. Colonies resident along the coastal section of the study area were most likely to occupy roost sites continuously, whereas traditional sites on the Atherton Tableland were only occupied on a recognisably winter or summer basis, without continuity.

A distinct pattern of movement between the Innisfail area and the southern Atherton Tableland has been inferred by roost-site occupancy data and some observations. Traditional roost sites were located within and at each end of the Palmerston Valley. Distances between the three roost sites along this suspected movement route (following the Johnstone River) were 36 and 12.5 kilometres. (In north-eastern New South Wales, grey-headed flying-fox movements of up to 100 kilometres have been shown to be strongly linked to watercourses.)

Differences in fruiting seasons and types of rainforest may have some influence on the occurrence of these seasonal migrations. The altitudinal difference between the coast and Atherton (over 700 metres) accounts for differences in rainforest species composition, as well as for differences in the fruiting seasons of species that are common to both regions. *Elaeocarpus angustifolius*, a species in the known diet of spectacled flying foxes, fruits in the lowland areas near Innisfail from May to August/September, but in areas above 300 metres (Kuranda) from August to December/early January.

It is possible that some colonies of spectacled flying foxes utilising a particular rainforest type may have to accommodate a greater variability in food supply, whereas others do not, especially during the young-rearing phase when energetic demands are high. In lowland areas, and possibly upland areas as well, the late dry-season months (August and September) constituted the period of overall peak fruiting in rainforest. The birth period of spectacled flying foxes lags this fruiting peak by one month. The late wet-season months (March to May) are the period of least fruit abundance, and this corresponds with the period when colonies left their traditional maternity roosts on the Atherton Tableland.

Migrations influenced by differential ripening of fruit also occur in the Torres Strait region north of Australia. This is an area located between Cape York and the New Guinea mainland and contains approximately 40 islands and atolls. There is strong evidence that black flying foxes leave New Guinea in September each year and progressively infiltrate islands southward, following the ripening of native fruits and exotics such as mangoes. By the following March these animals have disappeared from the area and are presumed to have returned to New Guinea.

MIGRATIONS BY NECTARIVOROUS SPECIES

Three recorded migrations by little red flying foxes to the Atherton Tableland, where they were not normally distributed, could be related to the apparent failure of inland eucalypt flowering. In general terms, the flowering phenology of *Eucalyptus* and *Corymbia* shows some degree of seasonality. The flowering times of these and other eucalypts in North Queensland are either throughout the winter or during the summer wet season. The consequences of either winter-flowering or summer-flowering species failing to produce a crop, and therefore not providing potential food for nomadic little red flying foxes, is such that if no flowering (or nectar production) occurs in winter species, then there is no carry-over of summer species to provide food. This causes major migrations of the bat to the Atherton Tableland. When this occurred, conditions in the Gulf Country were apparently detrimental to the survival of this species. At the time of two migrations (August 1984 and September 1986), apiarists harvesting from eucalypts in the Gulf Country complained of very low honey production.

During the 1986 migration, many little red flying foxes were seen to be emaciated, and were feeding during the day on blossom in public areas such as parks, and roosted in busy public areas within urban Atherton. One bat even fed in a low *Callistemon* shrub in a busy primary school yard, in amongst the students during the day. Apart from this unusual behaviour, another eight individuals in poor condition were found that had fallen out of such trees and died. At the time of this visit, a colony that arrived at another roost site was similarly affected, and approximately 40 dead individuals had fallen from trees over a six day period. This information indicates that these bats were already suffering from a food shortage prior to their arrival in September.

MIGRATIONS BY DIETARY GENERALISTS

Figure 9.1

The blossom of the grey ironbark (*Eucalyptus paniculata*) and the fruit of the lillypilly (*Acmenia smithii*) are both food to the dietary generalist grey-headed flying fox.

Long-distance migrations by flying foxes were suggested in early research, whereas more recent studies indicate that localised movement patterns are perhaps more typical. Recent work in New South Wales demonstrates that both long and short migrations occur during the annual cycle of grey-headed flying foxes. One of the implications of these movements is that there is a great deal of genetic interchange throughout eastern Australia within grey-headed, and perhaps black, flying foxes.

Studies in north-eastern New South Wales reveal a seasonal migration of grey-headed flying foxes from the coast to inland areas, which were attributed to both climate (temperature) and food availability. The influence of the weather is an as yet uninvestigated aspect of the ecology of flying foxes. There is some evidence to indicate that two races of grey-headed flying foxes may exist, separable by fur density and length: a southern (cold-adapted) form, and a northern (subtropical) form. However, there is stronger evidence that food availability is the driving force for movements and migrations of dietary generalist species.

As mentioned above, strong evidence from radio-tracking studies shows that colonies of grey-headed flying foxes have individuals that primarily select blossom, and others that primarily select fruit. Ten individuals from two separate roosts in north-eastern New South Wales were radio-tracked during nightly foraging and over a season. Those from one roost fed primarily on subtropical rainforest fruit and had annual movements between roosts of approximately 50 kilometres. Those from the other roost fed primarily on eucalypt flowers, and moved to other roosts up to 800 kilometres from their origin. One individual in the latter category moved 210 kilometres in three nights to a new feeding area. These annual differences in movement patterns reflect the variable fruiting and flowering phenology of forests in eastern Australia, and the progressively southward flowering of *Corymbia maculata* was found to be the predominant reason for migration.

The bare-backed flying fox has a very restricted distribution in far north-eastern Australia, being found on Cape York Peninsula, north of about Cooktown. The only known permanent camp of this large bat is in a massive boulder pile on the beach at the mouth of the Pascoe River near Iron Range. Information on the species consists of reports from short visits to this colony, and data from specimens collected from one or two other locations on Cape York. From their roost at the mouth of the Pascoe River, bare-backed flying foxes forage nightly as far away as Lockhart River, 30 kilometres to the south. They are frequently heard and caught in the rainforest at nearby Iron Range where they have been seen feeding in the understorey on cauliflorous flowers and fruit. They will also feed on the outer canopy flowers of eucalypts growing near rainforest, and have been seen feeding in a pawpaw tree in a backyard at Lockhart River.

Observations on tagged eastern tube-nosed fruit bats in northern Queensland have shown them to be resident in an area for several years. Tube-nosed bats are solitary roosters, and during the day hang in the mid to lower branches of trees where they mimic dead leaves. They generally roost in the same location for several days, and the roost will not be far away from a food source, such as a fruiting fig. When the food source is depleted, the bat moves its roost site to the vicinity of its next food tree. The asynchronous fruiting of figs (its main food source) allows this bat to utilise a patch of forest without needing to make seasonal migrations or long-distance movements away from the area. Since eastern tube-nosed fruit bats are found down the east coast to northern New South Wales, it is possible that different species of figs may cause different behavioural patterns to those observed in North Queensland.

The Queensland blossom bat has been recorded travelling up to 6 kilometres from its roost to feed. Roosts are usually located in the sub-canopy layer of dense forest adjacent to a feeding area, such as heathland. Sometimes rainforest trees with a dense canopy and growing in *Melaleuca* swamps are selected as roost sites. These roosts are changed frequently but the distance between consecutive roosts is usually less than 50 metres. In New South Wales some plant species, such as *Banksia integrifolia*, flower consistently for up to six months, and the bat shows great fidelity to these trees as a feeding site. Tagged individuals have been recorded turning up at the same tree at the same time on successive years, and have been recorded moving 30 kilometres between seasons.

CONSERVATION AND MANAGEMENT

Flying foxes, fruit bats and blossom bats are protected fauna in all states of Australia. In Queensland, a culling permit system is available for fruit growers who have to show that they have crop damage due to flying foxes. This was not always the case, and for the period 1985–94, flying foxes were removed from the protected fauna list in Queensland. Prior to 1985, flying foxes were not protected in New South Wales. It appears that during this period, when they were given 'pest' status, such severe damage was inflicted upon flying-fox populations that they may never recover to their previous numbers. Although they were protected, in New South Wales, the issuing of licences to cull in some areas may have resulted in the loss of at least 250 000 bats over an eight-year period (1986–92).

CURRENT POPULATION STATUS

Flying foxes were already suffering decreasing numbers when Francis Ratcliffe conducted his pioneering research in the late 1920s. Since then, there has been a continuation of decreasing populations. Possibly this is just as well, as there has been a concomitant loss of habitat during that period, and these two aspects are undoubtedly related. The effects of selective logging and the promotion of monocultural native timber forests would also have a deleterious effect on flying foxes. Much of the forest clearing has been done on fertile soils which would have provided trees with better and more reliable flowering and fruiting. Many of the forests that survived the clearing are on poor soils and produce poor amounts of nectar in flowers, and less and poorer quality fruit.

An estimate of the national population of grey-headed flying foxes in 1998 showed that there were less than 400 000. Yet eight years before this count was conducted, two camps alone were recorded in New South Wales that equalled this number. In the late 1920s, Francis Ratcliffe reported seeing numerous camps in south-east Queensland which alone exceeded the present national total. Even given the variation and reliability in counting flying foxes, it is obvious that a serious decline has occurred in the numbers of grey-headed flying foxes.

The northern rivers area of New South Wales, where flying foxes have caused problems with orchardists, was an area where there has been extensive removal of flying-fox food resources by land clearing. One example is the loss of the extensive rainforest tract known as the Big Scrub. The resulting large cleared pockets of land became barriers in times of bad flowering and nectar production: a dinner table with empty plates. The energy cost of using a region where patches of food are widely spaced can only have a deleterious effect, and due to the lack of their natural food, flying foxes become weak from 'fruitless searching', and turn to orchards for survival.

The culling of flying foxes has been severe in several areas, particularly in the Bega area of New South Wales in the early 1900s, and in the northern rivers area of New South Wales in the late 1980s. This culling was principally conducted by fruit growers and had an impact on flying-fox numbers. The raiding of orchards by flying foxes occurs when local flowering is poor. The combination of death from lack of natural food, plus the shooting and killing of hungry flying foxes at orchards, are the main contributors to the rapidly decreasing numbers of flying foxes in eastern Australia. Shooting, however, has been shown to be a totally ineffective method of orchard protection. Sometimes the flying foxes from the local camp are not the ones raiding orchards, since flying foxes can move long distances each night in search of food and frequently fly past other flying-fox camps on their nightly wanderings.

Figure 10.1
The fruit of the small-leafed fig (*Ficus obliqua*) are food to grey-headed and black flying foxes, and to eastern tube-nosed fruit bats. Clearing of these trees could affect all of these species' survival.

WHY CONSERVE FLYING FOXES, FRUIT BATS AND BLOSSOM BATS?

The most important reason for the conservation and management of Australian flying foxes is their undoubtedly important role in pollination and seed dispersal of Australian forest trees. The continued loss of populations of primary pollinators and seed dispersers can only have a long-term negative effect upon eucalypt forests in eastern Australia. Similarly, the continued commercial harvesting of such forests, conducted without consideration of the food requirements of flying foxes, possibly has a negative effect that is yet to be measured. This appears to be especially important in the light of the co-dependence between these bats and forest trees (see Chapter 8).

It is possible that some tree species dispersed only by flying foxes may be 'pivotal' species: that is they bear fruit during annual periods of otherwise fruit scarcity, and consequently maintain species of fruit-eating birds and mammals which are in turn critical for the dispersal and ultimate recruitment of many tree species at other times of the year. There is concern that some of the rainforest tree species that are dependent upon spectacled flying foxes for their seed dispersal, and hence for their successful reproduction, may also be pivotal species. The continued logging of rainforest in the range of this bat, concomitant with an apparent decline in their numbers, has far reaching long-term implications for maintaining the botanical diversity of this ecosystem.

The relationship between the Australian tube-nosed bats and the Queensland blossom bat with those from the same genera found in New Guinea (the centre of both groups' initial radiation) will provide important information on genetic rates of evolution. In addition, although they are known as fig specialists, tube-nosed fruit bats feed on a variety of other fruits in the forest, and could be shown to have special relationships with these plants. The ability of tube-nosed bats to distribute fig seeds over longer distances than birds and other mammals is important in fig biology. Both species of blossom bat are responsible for a certain amount of pollination in all the plants from which they obtain nectar. It has been shown that for one species of rainforest tree, blossom bats were the most effective pollinator, and the same situation is likely to be found for others.

MANAGEMENT PROBLEMS AND CONSIDERATIONS

On their negative side, flying foxes have an adverse effect on the fruit-growing industry, as well as upon the vegetation in their camp sites. They can cause considerable short-term damage to trees in their camp, and if the camp does not have enough area for the bats to move around and change their roost trees, long-term damage and death can occur to the vegetation.

One of the distinctive features of flying-fox ecology is their fidelity to established camp sites. Camp sites where young are born become especially significant to those animals, and they will continue to return to the camp, possibly for the rest of their lives. This desire to return and stay at a particular camp site is the main reason why most attempts to remove camp sites have failed.

Recently, flying foxes have been establishing camp sites close to, or in suburban areas. Camps which were once located in rural areas have also been overtaken by urban sprawl. This has led to problems with people who object to the noise, smell, tree damage, and droppings on clothes lines, cars and in swimming pools, and some types of flying-fox droppings will leave a permanent mark on painted objects and cars.

In Queensland this 'urbanisation' of flying foxes appears to be a purposeful choice by flying foxes, while in New South Wales it appears to be more a result of the ever increasing suburbia. The nearness of camps to houses gives protection from shooting, makes them easy to find at night because of street lights, and provides a reliable food resource, due to people watering their plants. There is evidence that some flying foxes are spending most of their time in urban areas. In south-east Queensland, the big camps of flying foxes containing 200 000–300 000 bats seen only 25 years ago have mostly disappeared and have been replaced by a number of smaller camps containing many less individuals, and often in an urban location. This has led to the misconception that flying foxes have actually increased in numbers in recent times.

Another feature of flying-fox ecology is their need to range over large areas when searching for food (as seen in Chapter 9). These movements can be overnight from a camp site, or over longer periods of up to several months and involve the use of a number of other camp sites. This requires a network of large areas of native forest throughout the flying fox's distribution. Different tree species flower at different times in different areas and many tree species have irregular flowering patterns.

This problem has been addressed in an extensive management report for flying foxes prepared in 1995 for the New South Wales National Parks and Wildlife Service. The management report suggested that objectives for management should shift from the control of the animals to the preservation of viable populations and the consideration of their pollination and seed dispersal functions. This shift in focus from control to conservation would also require a program of public education and participation in the development of government policy. Major recommendations of the management report revolved around:

- the cessation of culling programs on commercial crops that can be covered with netting to exclude these bats (which appears to be happening)
- the cessation of culling of flying foxes in their traditional roosts
- the development of techniques for deterring animals from establishing new camps in controversial areas.

MANAGEMENT — SPECIES BY SPECIES

There are unique problems in trying to devise a management plan for a mobile animal which has unpredictable movements and no concept of state or international boundaries. To add to these problems is the fact that each species has different ecological and behavioural patterns, and these can vary significantly between species. If just seasonal movements alone are considered, the problems of flying-fox management and conservation can be appreciated. The following accounts are brief summaries of the seasonal movements of Australian flying foxes relative to management problems and considerations. (This type of information is unfortunately lacking for the dusky flying fox, which is possibly extinct, and the bare-backed flying fox.)

LITTLE RED FLYING FOX

Regular and reasonably predictable movement patterns have been recorded for this species in the south-east Queensland/north-east New South Wales region, but may be different elsewhere. Seasonal movements in south-east Queensland and northern New South Wales see little reds coming in from the north and moving to coastal areas by late summer. They then slowly move up the coast and disappear inland until the next summer. Nightly moves in search of food are only up to 20–30 kilometres from their camp site. They appear to be more sedentary in the Northern Territory, where seasonal monsoons appear to promote regular flowering of eucalypts and melaleucas, and therefore a reliable food supply. Enormous colonies of over several million have been seen in the Gulf Country in Queensland. These large camps only appear every couple of years following good rain and may be important genetic mixers and essential for long-term survival of the species.

However, the general pattern in North Queensland is one of irregular and unpredictable movements: little reds are truly nomadic. Having to compete in this area with black and spectacled flying foxes, they spend most of the time in the dry tropical woodlands, but occasionally migrate to coastal regions, apparently when food is short elsewhere. Several of these migrations could be related to the flowering pattern of eucalypts, particularly winter-flowering species. If around four consecutive months of rainfall deficit occurs, the winter-flowering eucalypts apparently fail to provide nectar, and the bats have no food until the following summer. It is easy to imagine the size of the area required for this species in the Gulf, and how impossible it would be to establish a reserve network accordingly.

Continued wide-spread clearing in central Queensland has removed trees which were major winter and spring food sources for little reds. As a result, larger numbers of little reds are remaining on the central Queensland coast looking for alternative sources of food during this period. Unfortunately these include exotic cultivated fruit.

GREY-HEADED FLYING FOX

In the *Biology and Management of Flying Foxes in New South Wales* report of 1995, it is stated that when assessed as single, extensive populations without the legislative constraints of state boundaries, the conservation status of both black and little red flying foxes are apparently secure. The northern portions of their distribution contain extensive areas of relatively undisturbed forest which the species occupy consistently. Despite all this, there is cause for concern regarding the conservation status of grey-headed flying foxes. This species is vulnerable to extensive habitat loss and to human predation throughout its range. The inability to accurately assess their population size limits future monitoring programs to determination of trends in abundance.

The grey-headed flying fox undertakes irregular long-distance movements within its range from eastern Victoria to just north of Bundaberg, Queensland, and can travel up to 40 kilometres per night in search of food. These long-distance movements (for instance from Grafton to Nowra has been observed) are timed to take advantage of exceptional flowering and nectar production and are not a regular seasonal movement. Varying quantities of food cause grey-headed flying foxes to move from the Richmond River area, northern New South Wales, to south-eastern Queensland, and vice versa. The existing reserve system for the grey-headed flying fox in eastern Australia does not accommodate these highly mobile animals, and at the time of writing only 5 per cent of roost sites of this species were protected in reserves in New South Wales.

In New South Wales in 1991, less than 180 million square kilometres (or 12 per cent) of the remaining 1500 square kilometres of suitable native forests were in conservation reserves. In Queensland this value is only 84 square kilometres (7 per cent) of the remaining 1200 square kilometres. Recent extensions to the reserve network in New South Wales may have alleviated this problem slightly, but the issue still needs to be addressed.

Figure 10.2
Management considerations for the black flying fox include the fact that all outbreaks of Hendra virus have been within the range of this species and that the species regularly moves between Australia and New Guinea. Because they can be easily found in their daytime camps, black flying foxes are proving to be highly suitable for monitoring the environment. (Clancy Hall)

The concern about the decline in grey-headed flying-fox numbers, and the documented loss of major camps in northern New South Wales and south-east Queensland, has resulted in the species being listed nationally as 'vulnerable' in the national Bat Action Plan produced by the Federal Government Department, Environment Australia.

BLACK FLYING FOX

Detailed movement studies of this species in the Northern Territory show a seasonal pattern of camp occupation that is influenced by food resources as well as climatic conditions. Camps are made in bamboo and mangroves in the dry season, but use the shady areas of rainforest in the hot summer wet season. In the dry season they feed in eucalypt woodland, but switch to paperbarks and rainforest fruits in the wet. However, one of the most important results of this study was that only 3 per cent of recorded foraging or roosting locations were in any form of conservation reserve.

In Torres Strait there is a seasonal movement of black flying foxes where they follow the ripening of fruit on islands. In Queensland, anecdotal observations suggest that only short movements are made by black flying foxes, and these occur on a seasonal basis as animals move from one camp to another in search of food. These movements are local and no long-distance movements have been recorded. The Northern Territory study supports this speculation, as radio-tracking showed that nightly foraging movements rarely exceeded 20 kilometres in total, and most of the foraging was done less than 6 kilometres from the camp. The trend in the Northern Territory appears to be toward many smaller camps (less than 3000 individuals), whereas in Queensland, camps are larger (over 20 000), so foraging distances may be greater. This is further evidence that the conservation and management of this species (and others) must be planned at a major landscape level, and that a few conservation reserves would not be sufficient for their survival.

SPECTACLED FLYING FOX

This species has a pronounced seasonal movement from the warmer lowlands in winter to the high rainforest covered ranges in summer. This can be related to the later ripening of fruit in the uplands. Total distances covered are in the order of several hundred kilometres seasonally. Night-time foraging is local and near the camp site. All the factors have an effect on possible conservation and management programs for this species.

LARGE-EARED FLYING FOX

Although widespread in New Guinea, this species is currently known from only one Australian camp site near Boigu Island in Torres Strait.

It is probable that there is only several thousand animals within the nation, although other camps may be found after more exploration and survey in the area. Each night these bats leave the safety of their mangrove island camp in Queensland, and fly over to feed in the forests of the New Guinea mainland.

The conservation and management of this species will be a difficult problem, if not impossible, as its ecological patterns span two nations. The problems caused by international boundaries are further emphasised when comparisons are made between the status of the bat in the two countries. Due to its small and restricted population in Australia, the species is regarded as threatened, while 14 kilometres away in New Guinea they are regarded as numerous, and are hunted for food.

TORRESIAN FLYING FOXES

As far as can be determined, this species is restricted to Moa Island and perhaps nearby Badu Island in Torres Strait. It is also possible that this bat may be present on nearby Yam Island, which also has rainforest but has not as yet been surveyed for bats. Groups of 'small black flying-foxes' have been seen in camps of black flying foxes on Cape York Peninsula, but they have never been captured or properly identified. Night-time foraging trips are probably no longer than 20 kilometres, but most involve a flight of about 5 kilometres to the main patch of rainforest on the island. No seasonal movements of the bats to other camp sites or islands have been observed in this species, and it is present in its camp site on Moa Island during most times of the year. The conservation and management of this species is simplified by its remoteness and restriction to a unique area.

Figure 10.3
Radio tracking has revealed important information on the movements and feeding ecology of flying foxes. Here the authors (foreground) and Leon Hughes locate a Torresian flying fox in its daytime camp in a patch of mangroves on Moa Island, Torres Strait. (Pamela Conder)

BARE-BACKED FLYING FOXES

Little is known about the habitat requirements of the bare-backed fly-ing fox, which is restricted to northern coastal Cape York. Perhaps the most important factor in relation to their conservation and manage-ment is their daytime roosting in boulder caves and under rock over-hangs covered with vegetation, the only known permanent roost in Australia being at the mouth of the Pascoe River on Aboriginal con-trolled land near Iron Range. Due to the remote location of these roosts it would appear that the bare-backed flying fox has no immedi-ate management problems.

FRUIT BATS

Both tube-nosed fruit bats and blossom bats roost as solitary individu-als and do not form large congregations, as do flying foxes.

Much more research needs to be conducted on tube-nosed fruit bats before effective management plans can be drafted. The taxonomy of the group and the correct identity of the Australian forms is cur-rently under investigation. Surveys are needed to establish the full dis-tribution of the Cape York tube-nosed bat which is likely to be found in a larger area on Cape York than just around Silver Plains station near Coen. Further surveys should also show that the Torresian tube-nosed bat is not restricted to Moa Island. A list is needed of the trees on which these bats feed and subsequently disperse seeds.

Most of the ecological information on eastern tube-nosed fruit bats has come from research conducted at the Cape Tribulation Field Study Centre, located in lowland coastal rainforest which has been extensively cleared for agricultural purposes. Additional studies in the southern part of the distribution of this bat are required to provide information on movements and food trees. Long-term radio tracking and banding would provide important information on the size of forest patches needed to sustain viable populations of these bats.

Tube-nosed fruit bats are fig specialists, and the preservation of these trees is necessary for this bat's conservation and management. They have been recorded feeding on figs in forest along rivers and in disturbed regrowth areas, so they seem capable of utilising a range of habitats. Their acquired taste for introduced guavas (*Psidium gauja-va*), five-corner fruit (*Averroha carambola*), and soursops (*Annona muricata*) may develop into a management problem as more tropical orchards appear in Far North Queensland.

BLOSSOM BATS

blossom bats are reliant on nectar as a major food source, but both Australian species are known to eat some soft fruits as well. It is not known what effect fire in heathlands has on blossom bats, but severe fires could totally remove their food supply. Although seasonal movements of this bat are not fully understood, a reserve system embracing large areas of coastal heath with adjacent forest would be beneficial. The availability of rainforest as roosting habitat adjacent to feeding habitat is also important.

The Queensland blossom bat relies heavily on *Banksia* and *Melaleuca*, tree species which are common in coastal heath. It has been shown that while *Banksia* density was a poor predictor of Queensland blossom bat numbers, the number of productive inflorescences on trees and the amount of nectar were good predictors. This has important conservation implications, as a direct relationship between loss of feeding habitat and numbers of bats can be made. The clearing of coastal vegetation for development, plus the invasion of heath and littoral rainforest by introduced weeds such as bitou bush, are serious threats to Queensland blossom bats.

The Queensland blossom bat has also been the subject of some excellent research in coastal New South Wales where it tends to be a heathland specialist. This habitat preference also occurs in south-east Queensland, but in north Queensland the bat is found in a variety of habitats including rainforest. Equivalent studies need to be conducted in northern Queensland. It is likely that management strategies for this species will vary significantly between the two states and will involve a different suite of considerations.

Very little research has been conducted on the northern blossom bat in Australia, and most information has come from collected specimens. (An extensive study on the species has been conducted in Malaysia.) It is a frequent visitor to flowering bananas in northern Queensland, but since bananas self-pollinate, the northern blossom bat does not have a role in their pollination.

It is not known if there are any specific native plants that are used by the northern blossom bat for feeding, but it has been caught in flowering paperbarks (*Melaleuca cajuputi*) and the freshwater mangrove (*Barringtonia acutangula*) in the Northern Territory. Its long pointed snout, brush tongue, and highly reduced dentition suggest that there may be some special plant relationships with this bat, yet to be revealed.

MANAGEMENT OPTIONS AND METHODS

As mentioned, management practices should consider the widespread regional scale, even including neighbouring countries, but should also account for bats at a local level. Obvious localised problems include management around orcharding districts, and the negative interactions with humans as a result of camp locations.

Broad-scale management

Several species of flying fox which regularly cross international boundaries may present other management problems. These species are the black and large-eared flying foxes, which travel between New Guinea and Queensland. One implication here is the possible introduction of screw-worm fly, which would be devastating to the beef industry, and possibly viral diseases. It is probable that other species of New Guinean flying foxes are also involved in movements in the Cape York–Torres Strait area. There is a record from the 1980s of a 'huge flying fox with a yellowish head, neck and back' from Thursday Island, which it is suspected could only be a vagrant Bismarck flying fox (*Pteropus neohibernicus*) from New Guinea.

It is extremely difficult for fauna authorities to develop a reserve system that will accommodate the often unpredictable movements of flying foxes. The irregular flowering nature of eucalypts and the climatic influence of El Niño and Southern Oscillation Index are yet to be fully understood in relation to flying-fox ecology. The Regional Forest Agreement signed by state and Commonwealth governments is designed to establish a comprehensive, adequate and representative reserve system throughout Australian forests. Particular attention will be focused on threatening processes of human-induced disturbance, and how this affects the susceptibility to extinction of different forest-dependent species such as flying foxes. It is hoped that this initiative will see the establishment of the reserve system that is necessary if flying foxes are to survive.

Rehabilitation of our landscapes under these programs, and the new efforts by the timber industry to farm their resource in plantations, should include tree species favoured by flying foxes. Collaboration such as this, where one industry (timber) would be passively assisting another (fruit production), whilst also assisting with wildlife conservation that includes flying foxes, would be an excellent partnership. It should be noted that not just flying foxes would be assisted, but also the many other vertebrates that feed on eucalypt flowers, the honey industry, plus the large number of animals that use forests in other ways.

Managing camps

In terms of local management plans or strategies, it would seem that an obvious place to start with flying foxes is at their camp sites. Currently this is an area where humans and flying foxes are coming into conflict, and there is a long history of humans attempting to move or eradicate flying-fox camps. The notion of removing flying-fox camps totally from a site in eastern Australia should be discouraged completely. The numbers of flying foxes have decreased sufficiently in eastern Australia to cause seriously worry about their long-term survival. Camp sites need to be maintained and managed, not destroyed.

Most previous efforts to remove camps have been abject failures, mainly because the people involved have not used any knowledge of flying-fox ecology. Their attempts are more akin to insect pest control methods, and do not make an effort to educate the public about the important role that flying foxes play in the environment. The involvement of the media and uninformed people who have political and other agendas, has caused a number of attempts amounting to a public farce. They have been costly, often barbaric (for instance the use of flame-throwers and explosives), illogical in concept, and do not reflect well on the Australian nation.

Flying foxes are intelligent animals and will move camp if continually harassed by human activity under their roosting trees, and by the use of loud noise and smoke. In many cases this has resulted in flying foxes settling in a new area which is even less desirable (to humans) than the original camp site. As soon as the disturbance has ceased, the flying foxes will return to their original camp. During the disturbance, some flying foxes that use the camp site could be hundreds of kilometres away searching for food, and as soon as local flowering is good, these animals will return. Nobody will have told them that their camp site was now out of bounds.

The very few successful attempts at camp removal occurred when there was another suitable alternate camp site nearby, or when the disturbance coincided with the time when local flowering was finishing and flying foxes were moving from the area on their own accord. Even then, the success of the removal in the long term is not guaranteed. Flying foxes will always return to a known camp site, even years later, when local tree flowering is good. The total removal of all trees at a camp site will, of course, mean that flying foxes abandon the site. However, they will probably move to a less favourable site and become someone else's problem, and will eventually return to the original camp site when trees have regrown. Tree removal would have to be regarded as a pathetic and desperate wildlife control method. This further emphasises that long-term camp removal is a futile exercise, and that camp management is the more sensible procedure.

Management of flying-fox camp sites involves minimising conflicts between flying foxes and hostile local residents. This can be achieved by expanding (planting) roosting trees for flying foxes in areas away from such residents, and then making the area near the residents less attractive. This is achieved by clearing all the understorey, bushes and vines from under the trees, and lopping branches from some of the taller trees. This creates a more open forest environment, a vegetation type that is rarely used by flying foxes. Quick-growing bushy acacias, in which flying foxes seldom roost, can be planted along residents' back fences to further screen the colony if necessary.

This approach has been successfully practised by Ipswich City Council at the suburban Woodend Nature Reserve. After realising the futility of trying to move the flying foxes, Ipswich Council formed a flying-fox advisory group. The group was composed of local residents, members of the council, wildlife authorities and researchers. A management plan was developed and the council embarked on a tree planting program to expand the flying-fox camp away from back yards. Within five years, quick-growing tree species were being used as roosting sites by the flying foxes away from the back yards.

Flying-fox camps that have been used by large numbers over periods of time usually have enough vegetation and space for the flying foxes to move their roosting areas within the camp. However, many flying-fox camps need to be expanded to lessen the damage to vegetation caused by roost in the same tree for long periods of time. Once young are born in a camp, the camp site becomes a permanent fixture in their geographical memory and they will continue to return to the camp. Recently, new flying-fox camp sites have appeared in a number of localities. Sometimes these are actually old camp sites which have not been used for a long time. The appearance of these camps is usually the result of good flowering by local eucalypts. The possibility of planting trees in suitable areas (such as protected valleys) to attract flying foxes could be encouraged.

Education of not only school children but the general public as well should be a high priority in flying-fox conservation and management. Much of the dislike for flying foxes comes from ignorance and superstition, and bad media coverage. The media sensationalises items of flying-fox news (and all bats in general) to promote their sales or viewing. There is ample information on the unique and important role flying foxes play in our environment to include them in our national school education programs.

MANAGEMENT AROUND ORCHARDS

There have been many attempts to prevent flying foxes from raiding orchards. If they are desperately short of their natural food, very few techniques will prevent these intelligent animals from getting to the fruit. Bright lights, gas guns and an amazing variety of unsuccessful techniques have been tried. Recently, a new system for passively excluding flying foxes from orchards has been developed and is being tested. This new system combines 'surround sound' at low frequencies to create a zone of discomfort for the animals, with the use of recorded distress calls and gun blasts, which are randomly selected by a computer to prevent flying foxes getting used to them.

There has been an interesting twist to the fruit growers' problem with flying foxes. The design of bat-proof and ultraviolet-proof netting for orchards has produced a product which also keeps out all other large fruit-eating pests (such as birds, possums and rats), provides protection from wind and hail, and produces a microclimate under cover which yields superior fruit. So the flying foxes have done the orchardists a favour! Although netting is expensive, and not always suited to every orchard, discussions with growers suggest it is cost-effective in the long term, particularly when establishing an orchard or replanting. Other problems with netting are being investigated by the Queensland Department of Primary Industries.

However, orchard exclusion systems are merely a band-aid for a problem that requires a major operation, and do not address the reasons why these animals are raiding the crops in the first place. There are national efforts in place to restore vegetation, particularly in eastern coastal Australia where the habitat loss within the distributional range of flying foxes has been greatest, and includes initiatives from Greening Australia, Land care groups, and the Billion Trees Program.

HUMAN USE AND INTERACTION PAST AND PRESENT

FLYING FOXES AS FOOD

In the early days of colonisation in Australia there were many people who led a subsistence lifestyle. These people often relied heavily on their fruit trees and regularly shot flying foxes that raided their orchards. This persistent shooting was so severe in several areas — such as around Bega, New South Wales, and Byfield, Queensland — that flying foxes became locally rare. Today, some problems still exist with fruit growers, but it has been clearly shown that netting of orchards not only excludes flying foxes, but other orchard pests, as well as preventing wind and hail damage.

On the island of Guam, two species of flying foxes were traditionally harvested as a source of red meat. Over-harvesting occurred to the extent that one species is now extinct and the other has been reduced to such low numbers that it also faces extinction. It has been suggested that Australian flying foxes could be harvested and supplied to the Melanesians to prevent further illegal harvesting of their local flying foxes. With their low reproductive rate, decreasing numbers and often severe natural mortalities, harvesting of Australian flying foxes would seem most unwise and certainly not sustainable.

That another country has exterminated their own flying foxes by harvesting indicates that there is no such thing as sustainable harvesting. The supplying of Australian flying foxes to another country which

has exterminated its own species is a retrograde step in wildlife management and conservation, and probably only serves to line the pockets of a small number of business people. A previous investigation into
the possibility of harvesting flying foxes showed that a harvest rate of
only 10 per cent per year reduced the population by 90 per cent in 20
years. This study did not include the possibility of killing pregnant
females when harvesting.

The only flying-fox populations large enough to be considered for
harvesting in Australia are those found in the Gulf Country of
Queensland, the Northern Territory and the Kimberly region of
Western Australia. In these areas females have extended breeding
seasons, and at any one time of the year females in a camp are
involved in some stage of their reproductive cycle. Also, in most of
this area, flying foxes do not cause problems with fruit growers or
have camps in inappropriate sites. In addition, the finding of several
viruses in Australian flying foxes makes it unlikely that any country
would want to import them for human consumption. Before harvesting should be considered, the absolute minimum requirement needed is research to enable a properly constructed life history table so
the effects of harvesting can be predicted. It is highly unlikely that
this knowledge would support harvesting.

USEFULNESS TO SCIENCE

In Aboriginal communities in northern Queensland, the Torres Strait
and in the Northern Territory, flying foxes are traditionally recommended eating as a cure for people with respiratory problems, particularly children. The same folklore for feeding flying foxes to people
with respiratory illness is widespread throughout much of New
Guinea, Indonesia and South-East Asia, and warrants further medical
investigation.

The recent emergence of viruses such as Hendra and Lyssavirus,
and their relationship with humans, domestic animals and flying foxes,
indicates that flying foxes will play an important role in the detection,
surveillance and monitoring of emerging diseases.

There is some merit in trying to utilise carcasses of flying foxes shot
at orchards and camps by fruit growers, possibly for human consumption or research. In the past, fruit growers have been unco-operative in
advising or allowing access to flying foxes shot in orchards, or at nearby camps. This has prevented the collection of important information
on sex and age structure of flying-fox camps, and which ones are raiding orchards. This type of information could have made an important
contribution to our knowledge of flying foxes, and been used for their
management.

Due to their body size, relative ease of feeding and housing, flying foxes have also become a popular research and zoo animal. One aspect of their biology which has probably influenced their use as an experimental animal is their slow breeding rate, with the production of only one offspring per year. To counter their slow breeding rate however, flying foxes have a long life-span in captivity, with records of animals surviving for over 30 years.

A large captive colony of flying foxes at the University of Queensland established by Dr Len Martin has provided animals for some very innovative research and is currently being used for virus and eye research. Although using flying foxes as the primary study animal, this research has often had wider application to our under-standing of concepts in areas such as neurophysiology, reproduction, and flight mechanics. (See references to Bennett; Calford; Martin; O'Brien; and Pettigrew.)

Many zoos and environmental parks now have flying foxes on dis-play. There are also a number of people who have tame flying foxes, and regularly display them to school children and groups. Since the finding of a number of dangerous viruses in flying foxes, their use in public dis-play has become less popular, and public health regulations for han-dling flying foxes requires special care (see Chapter 11). There is an urgent need to develop a means to inoculate flying foxes against these viruses so that animals can be used for public display and education.

TOURISM

With the absence of flying foxes in their countries, the large numbers of North American, Japanese and European tourists find a camp of large noisy bats hanging out in the open a most interesting place to visit. Visits to flying-fox camps by tourists, natural history and eco-tour groups are becoming a popular activity. If controlled, this use of flying-fox camps should form a good example of a sustainable eco-tourist activity. It is important that eco-tour guides are properly informed about the unique and important ecological role played by flying foxes in the Australian environment.

'Batty Boat' trips on Brisbane River have been run since 1983 as a fund-raising activity and to promote flying foxes. Over 8000 people, and numerous local and overseas television and documentary crews, have taken the trip to see the flying-fox camp and its fly-out from Indooroopilly Island. A number of Brisbane-based eco-tour operators are now running similar tours. Observation platforms have been built at flying-fox camps at Ku-ring-gai and Wingham Brush in New South Wales, and Woodend (Ipswich) and Hervey Bay in Queensland. These sites have become popular with international tourists. Many of the peo-ple visiting these camps are locals who want to get a closer look at an animal they usually see only as a silhouette in the late evening sky.

CHAPTER 11

REHABILITATION AND REARING

In the last ten years, the public interest in raising orphaned young or caring for injured flying foxes has grown to such an extent that there are more people involved in flying-fox care than those for any other species of native animal being rehabilitated in Australia. Stemming from this has been the use of flying foxes in educational programs. The potential to use flying foxes for educational purposes was first realised by these rehabilitators. However, the recent finding of several flying-fox viruses dangerous to man has made it necessary to re-evaluate the use of flying foxes for public display.

FEEDING AND CARING FOR INJURED ADULTS

Adult flying foxes are subject to a number of misadventures which can leave them in a state where human care, for a short period of time, is necessary for their survival and return to the wild. Getting their wings caught on the top strand of barbed-wire fences, lead poisoning, wing damage (rips, burns, and breaks) from aerial wires and power lines, physical weakness from periods of food shortage, tick infestations, and eating the green fruit of the widespread Queen palm

(*Syagrus romanzoffiana*) are some of the causes of flying foxes coming into human care.

Bats caught on barbed-wire fences and found under power lines are often weak and in a very bad physical condition, particularly if they have been there for some time and have been harassed by other animals. However, they can also be very aggressive, and it is recommended the people picking up injured bats, or removing them from fences, use leather gloves or a thick towel.

Wing rips, tears, and holes are best left to heal themselves, and this happens in a remarkably short time. Broken wings require pinning by a veterinarian. A suitable anaesthetic is a xylazine/ketamine mixture at a dose rate 0.1–0.2 millilitres per kilogram. This lasts for about 30 minutes. Halothane gas has also been successfully used to anaesthetise flying foxes with the machine set at 2 per cent and 2 litres. Broken thumbs are a critical injury. The loss of a thumb is a serious handicap for a flying fox, and although they will survive without one thumb, the loss will severely degrade the animal's lifestyle.

There is some evidence that bats that have fallen to misadventure could have had their normal faculties suppressed by disease. It is important that care be taken not to be scratched or bitten by these bats. If a deep bite or scratch occurs, the wound should be immediately washed with soapy water and the bat sent in for testing for Australian bat Lyssavirus and Hendra virus through a local veterinarian, health department, or state primary industries or agriculture department. (See Information box, page 111.)

Adult flying foxes are easy to keep in captivity, but require the appropriate permit from the state's fauna authority to do so. Most wildlife care groups and veterinarians have their own preferred method of feeding and raising flying foxes, and few are the same. These people should be contacted (see Information box, page 111) for advice if an orphaned or injured flying fox comes into your care.

The following information is provided as a general guide:

- Flying foxes eat most fruit and like bananas, pears, pawpaws, rock melons, peaches, grapes and tropical fruits. Apples and citrus are only eaten when there is no choice.
- When fruit is being fed to captive flying foxes it is necessary to add a protein and vitamin supplement to the food. About 10 grams of powdered milk should be sprinkled over the fruit, and this should be doubled if the animal is pregnant or lactating.
- If possible, it is good to include branches of flowering eucalypts, grevilleas, melaleucas, figs and so on, as these represent flying foxes' natural food.
- Flying foxes will also eat a small amount of green foliage, such as mulberry leaves.

- Flying foxes need to be fed fresh food daily, and water at all times. The addition of a small amount of table salt to their water seems to be appreciated.
- Cages need to be wide enough for flying foxes to stretch their wings, and tall enough so that the head is not hanging too close to the floor. The standard cockatoo cage is close to the minimum size for an adult flying fox.

Captive flying foxes are prone to a wing infection called 'slimy wing'. The principal cause of slimy wing appears to be the yeast fungus *Candida* and if not treated promptly will cause permanent and serious damage, and ultimately death. In mild cases the wings should be thoroughly washed with the dog wash Malaseb diluted one part to 30 parts water. In serious cases a veterinarian will be needed to administer a course of antibiotics. Several cases of slimy wing have been seen in wild flying foxes, but most cases involve captive animals which do not receive sufficient direct sunlight during the day.

RAISING ORPHANED YOUNG

The majority of young orphaned flying foxes are ones which are dropped from their mothers while they are out feeding at night. Females carry their young all the time for the first three weeks after birth, and this is quite a burden. These mothers frequently get electrocuted while trying to dodge power lines. When their wings touch two wires of overhead powerlines, they get a shock of 11 000 volts. Heat generated by the electricity is frequently transferred to the milk in the mouth of the young, resulting in burning. Strong winds at night also cause females to loose their young. Unfortunately females carrying young are shot at orchards, and the young sometimes survive. Shooting at orchards in mid- to late summer leaves numbers of orphaned young back in the camp site, where they perish unless rescued.

As with adults, it is necessary to have a permit to keep and raise young orphan flying foxes. There are a number of groups who run a network of carers for orphaned young native animals throughout all states. If you would like to raise a young flying fox, or if you find an orphaned young and wish to care for it, contact one of the groups which are listed in the Information box. These groups have the appropriate fauna permits, and have produced a number of books on the care of orphan young. They also have essential equipment for raising young, such as teats and heating pads.

Information: Help and information for the care of injured or orphaned bats

For problems, identification, or inquires related to flying foxes, fruit bats and blossom bats (or bats in general), contact the local branch of state departments of Conservation and Environment, or Parks and Wildlife. Local branches can be located in telephone directories. These authorities often have their own wildlife rehabilitation centres, or will provide information on who to contact. They are not always available out of office hours or on weekends. The following contacts deal specifically with injured or orphaned flying foxes, as well as other bats:

Far North Queensland
Wildlife Rescue, Cairns
ph. (07) 4053 4467

Orphan Native Animal Rear
and Release Program, Brisbane
ph (07) 3375 4620

Flying-fox Information and
Conservation Network, Nimbin
ph (02) 6649 2572

Ku-ring-gai Bat Conservation
Society, Sydney
ph (02) 9636 2251

There is an extensive network of additional wildlife and bat care groups which extend all over Queensland, New South Wales and Victoria. These groups have a good knowledge of local wildlife species, have relevant permits and can be contacted through the regional groups listed above.

Remember: Permits are necessary to keep any bats in captivity.

There have been a number of milk substitutes successfully used for rearing young flying foxes. Advice on the use of different milk types is given in carer handbooks, listed in References. As an emergency stop-gap until proper advice can be obtained, young bats can be fed every two to three hours on the 'Wombaroo' flying-fox milk mix, available from most veterinarians, or a mixture of one scoop of 'Nan' baby formula (available from supermarkets) to 25 millilitres of water. The milk should be 'wrist warm', and fed to the young from a small teat or dropper.

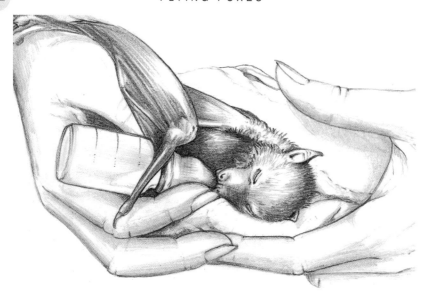

Figure 11.1
When feeding orphaned flying foxes, it is important, as with human babies, to check that the milk temperature is at body temperature.

WEANING

The natural growth rate of flying foxes is rapid. In three months they will have grown to over half adult weight, and attained adult proportions. By this stage they will also have gained many of the skills necessary for survival.

It is important to realise that humans are incapable of teaching a young flying fox how to be a flying fox! Unfortunate instances where flying foxes have dropped from the night sky onto unsuspecting people are probably the result of a hand-raised animal not being properly rehabilitated before its release. With the current knowledge of viruses in flying foxes, this is a highly undesirable situation.

One of the success stories of raising flying-fox young was the recognition of the importance of the young being educated before release back into the wild. This technique involves the gathering of foster-young from carers from an age when they would normally be about to become independent (at about 13–15 weeks, or with a forearm length of 12 centimetres) and placing them in a 'release cage' with several tame adult bats. The young are then exposed to these bats as well as to wild bats which visit the cage.

Their induction into the real world of flying foxes involves learning complex social behaviour through both visual and olfactory observation. Many young bats, who think that they are humans in flying-fox costumes, are terrified when they are first confronted by one of the adult flying foxes. In the release cages, the adults (usually a male) round up the young and protect them from aggressive behaviour, particularly from 'wild' animals on the outside of the cage.

After two weeks the doors of the cage are left open, with the young free to come and go when they please. Food is provided for another two weeks, by which time most of the bats have left. The most successful of the release cages are located near established flying-fox camps. It is important that young flying foxes be released back into the wild in the same area where they were found. This will prevent any unusual genetic mixing of the species, or releasing of flying foxes into areas outside of their normal range.

Large numbers of flying foxes are raised annually in Australia by this method. Returns from animals banded or micro-chipped on their release show healthy growth rates and integration back into colonies. It is important that all orphaned young are raised in this manner.

APPENDIX:
NATIVE PLANT SPECIES KNOWN TO BE CONSUMED BY AUSTRALIAN FLYING FOXES

Key

Plant part consumed
Fr = fruits
Fl = flowers
Fo = foliage

Flying-fox species
Pp = Pteropus poliocephalus
Pa = P. alecto
Ps = P. scapulatus
Pc = P. conspicillatus
Pb = P. banakrisi
Pm = P. macrotis

Sources
1 = Richards (1990)
2 = Parry-Jones and Augee (1991)
3 = Information from the Ku-ring-gai Bat Conservation Society
4 = Authors' observations

Plant species	Common name	Plant part consumed	Flying-fox species	Source
Achronychia acidula	rutaceae	Fr	Pc	1
Acmena smithii	lillypilly	Fr	Pp	3
Albizzia lebbek	white sirrus	Fl	Pa	4
A. procera	safe sirrus	Fo	Pc	1
Alphitonia excelsa	red ash	Fr	Pp	3
Angophora costata	smooth-barked apple	Fl	Pa, Pp	2, 4
A. floribunda	rough-barked apple	Fl	Pp	2
A. subvenlutina	rough-barked apple	Fl	Ps	4
Archontophoenix alexandrae	phoenix palm	Fr	Pc	1
A. cunninghamiana	bangalow palm	Fr	Pp	2, 3
Avicennia marina	grey mangrove	Fo	Pp	2
Banksia integrifolia	coast banksia	Fl	Pp	2, 3
B. serrata	old man banksia	Fl	Pp	2, 3
Callistemon citrinus	crimson bottlebrush	Fl	Pp	3
C. salignus	white bottlebrush	Fl	Pp	3
Canarium muelleri	scrub turpentine	Fr	Pc	1
Castanospermum australe	black bean	Fl	Pc, Pp	1, 3
Cissus hypoglauca	water vine	Fr	Pp	2, 3
Cocos nucifera	coconut palm	Fl	Pa, Pb, Pm	4
Corymbia citriodora	lemon scented gum	Fl	Pa, Pc, Pp, Ps	1, 4
C. eximia	yellow bloodwood	Fl	Pp	3
C. gummifera	red bloodwood	Fl	Pp	2, 3
C. henryi	spotted gum	Fl	Pa, Pp, Ps	4
C. intermedia	pink bloodwood	Fl	Pa, Pc, Pp, Ps	1, 4
C. maculata	spotted gum	Fl	Pp	2, 3
C. polycarpa	large-fruited bloodwood	Fl	Pa, Pc, Ps	1, 4
C. ptychocarpa	swamp bloodwood	Fl	Pa, Ps	4
C. torrelliana	cadagi	Fl	Pa, Pc, Pp	4
Decaspermum humile	myratceae	Fr	Pc	1
Dendrocnide excelsa	giant stinging tree	Fr	Pp	2, 3
Diploglottis australis	native tamarind	Fr	Pp	3
Ehretia acuminata	koda	Fr	Pp	3
Elaeocarpus angustifolius	quandong	Fr	Pc	1
E. bancrofti	quandong	Fr	Pc	1
E. obovatus	hard quandong	Fr	Pp	3
Eucalyptus acmenoides	white mahogany	Fl	Pa, Pp, Ps	4
E. alba	poplar gum	Fl	Pa, Ps	4
E. albens	white box	Fl	Pp	3

E. andrewsi	New England blackbutt	Fl	Pp	3
E. baileyana	Bailey's stringybark	Fl	Pa, Pp	4
E. blakelyi	Blakely's red gum	Fl	Pp	3
E. botyroides	southern mahogany	Fl	Pp	3
E. camaldulensis	river red gum	Fl	Pa, Ps	4
E. cloeziana	gympie messmate	Fl	Pa, Pc, Pp, Ps	1, 4
E. crebra	narrow-leaved ironbark	Fl	Pa, Pp	4
E. curtisii	Plunkett mallee	Fl	Pp	4
E. dealbata	hill gum	Fl	Pp	3
E. fastigata	brown barrel	Fl	Pp	4
E. fibrosa	broad-leaved ironbark	Fl	Pp	3
E. globoidea	white stringybark	Fl	Pp	4
E. grandis	flooded gum	Fl	Pa, Pp	4
E. longifolia	woollybutt	Fl	Pp, Ps	4
E. melanophloia	silver-leaved ironbark	Fl	Ps	4
E. melliodora	yellow box	Fl	Pp	3
E. microcorys	tallowwood	Fl	Pa, Pp	4
E. microtheca	coolibah	Fl	Ps	4
E. miniata	Darwin woollybutt	Fl	Pa, Ps	4
E. moluccana	grey box	Fl	Pp	3
E. obliqua	messmate stringybark	Fl	Pp	4
E. paniculata	grey ironbark	Fl	Pp	3
E. papuana	ghost gum	Fl	Pa, Ps	4
E. parramattensis	Parramatta gum	Fl	Pp	3
E. pilularis	blackbutt	Fl	Pa, Pp	3, 4
E. planchoniana	needlebark stringybark	Fl	Pp, Ps	4
E. propinqua	small-fruited grey gum	Fl	Pa, Pp	3, 4
E. punctata	large-fruited grey gum	Fl	Pp	3
E. racemosa	southern scribbly gum	Fl	Pp	3
E. radiata	narrow-leaved peppermint	Fl	Pp	4
E. resinifera	red mahogany	Fl	Pp	3, 4
E. robusta	swamp mahogany	Fl	Pa, Pp, Ps	2, 4
E. saligna	bluegum	Fl	Pa, Pp	3, 4
E. sieberi	silvertop ash	Fl	Pp	4
E. tereticornis	forest red gum	Fl	Pa, Pc, Pp, Ps	1, 4
E. tessellaris	Moreton Bay ash	Fl	Pa, Pp, Ps	4
E. tetrodonta	Darwin stringy bark	Fl	Pa, Ps	4
E. umbra	white mahogany	Fl	Pa, Pp, Ps	4
E. viminalis	ribbon gum	Fl	Pp	4
Faradaya splendida	liane	Fr	Pc	1
Ficus coronata	sandpaper fig	Fr	Pa, Pp	3, 4
F. crassipes	fig	Fr	Pc	1

F. fraseri	sandpaper fig	Fr	Pc, Pp	1, 3
F. macrophylla ·	Moreton Bay fig	Fr	Pa, Pp	3, 4
F. obliqua	small-leaved fig	Fr	Pa, Pp	3, 4
F. pleurocarpa	fig	Fr	Pc	1
F. rubiginosa	Port Jackson fig	Fr	Pp	3
F. triradiata	fig	Fr	Pc	1
F. virens	banyan	Fr	Pc	1
F. watkinsiana	strangler fig	Fr	Pp, Pc	1, 4
Grevillea pteridifolia	orange grevillia	Fl	Pa, Ps	4
G. robusta	silky oak	Fl	Pa, Pc, Pp	1, 2, 3, 4
Hedycarya angustifolia	native mulberry	Fr	Pp	3
Livistonia australis	cabbage palm	Fr	Pp	2
Lophostemon confertatus	brush box	Fl	Pa, Pp	3, 4
L. suaveolans	swamp box	Fl	Pa, Pp	4
Maclura cochinchinensis	cockspur thorn	Fr	Pp	2, 3
Mallotus discolor	white kamala	Fr	Pp	3
Manilkara kauki	wongai plum	Fr	Pa, Pb, Pc	1, 4
Melaleuca argentea	silver-leaved paperbark	Fl	Pa, Ps	4
M. leucodendron	weeping paperbark	Fl	Pa, Ps	4
M. quinquenervia	broad-leaved paperbark	Fl	Pa, Pp, Ps	2, 3, 4
M. viridiflora	green-flowering paperbark	Fl	Pa	4
Melia azederach	white cedar	Fr	Pc	1
Melodinus australis	apocynaceae	Fr	Pp	2
Morinda jasminoides	rubiaceae	Fr	Pp	2
Nauclea orientalis	Leichhardt tree	Fr	Pc	1
Neolitsea dealbata	bolly gum	Fl	Pc	1
Notothixos cornifolius	Kurrajong mistletoe	Fr	Pp	3
Parinari nonda	Nonda plum	Fr	Pa, Pb, Pc	1
Pittosporum undulatum	sweet pittosporum	Fl, Fr	Pp	2
Planchonella australis	black apple	Fr	Pp	3
Polyalthia michaeli	mast tree	Fr	Pc	1
Schizomeria ovata	cunoniaceae	Fr	Pp	2
Stenocarpus sinuatus	firewheel tree	Fl	Pp	3
Syncarpia glomulifera	turpentine	Fl	Pp, Pc	1, 2, 3, 4
Syzygium australe	brush cherry	Fr	Pp	3
S. dictyophllebium	lillypilly	Fr	Pc	1
S. forte	lillypilly	Fl	Pc	1
S. kuranda	Kuranda lillypilly	Fr	Pc	1
S. wesa	lillypilly	Fr	Pc	1
S. oleosum	blue lillypilly	Fr	Pp	3, 4
Terminalia arenicola	okari	Fr	Pc	1
T. catappa	beach almond	Fr	Pa, Pb, Pc, Pm	1, 4
T. sericocarpa	sovereignwood	Fr	Pc	1

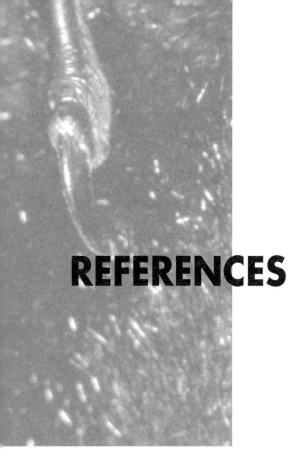

REFERENCES

Chapter 1 Introduction

Churchill S, *Australian Bats*, Reed/New Holland, Sydney, 1998.

Hill JE and Smith JD, *Bats: A natural history*, British Museum (Natural History), London, 1984.

Kunz TH and Racey PA (eds), *Bat biology and conservation*, Smithsonian Institution Press, Washington, 1998.

Menkhorst PW (ed), *Mammals of Victoria: Distribution, ecology and conservation*, Oxford University Press, Melbourne, 1995.

Richarz K and Limbrunner A, *The world of bats* (English trans TFH Publications Neptune City), New Jersey, 1993.

Strahan R (ed), *Mammals of Australia*, Reed, Sydney, 1995.

Walton DW and Richardson BJ (eds), *Fauna of Australia*, vol. 1B, *Mammals*, Bureau of Fauna and Flora, Canberra, 1989.

Wilson DE, *Bats in Question: The Smithsonian answer book*, Smithsonian Institution Press, Washington, 1997.

Chapter 2 Historical background

Archer M, Hand SJ and Godthelp H, *Riversleigh: The story of animals in ancient rainforests of inland Australia*, Reed Books, Sydney, 1991.

Hall LS, 'And then there were bats', in Archer M and Clayton G (eds), *Vertebrate zoogeography and evolution in Australasia: Animals in space and time*, Hesperian Press, Perth, 1984: pp 837–52.

——, 'Biogeography of Australian bats', in Keast A (ed), *Ecological biogeography of Australia*, W Junk, The Hague, 1981: pp 1557–83.

Hand S, 'Bat beginnings and biogeography: a southern perspective', in Archer M and

Clayton G (eds), *Vertebrate zoogeography and evolution in Australasia: Animals in space and time*, Hesperian Press, Perth, 1984: pp 853–904.

Mickleburgh SP, Hutson AM and Racey PA, *Old World fruit bats: An action plan for their conservation*, Chiroptera Specialist Group, Species Survival Commission, International Union for the Conservation of Nature, Switzerland, 1992.

Pettigrew JD, Jamieson BGM, Robson SK, Hall LS and McNally KI, 'Phylogenetic relationships microbats, megabats and primates: Mammalia, Chiroptera and Primates', *Philosophical Transactions of the Royal Society of London*, (Series B) 325, 1989: pp 489–559.

Ratcliffe F, *Flying fox and drifting sand*, Angus and Robertson, Sydney, 1947.

Wilson DE and Graham GL, 'Pacific Island flying-foxes', Proceedings of an International Conservation Conference, *Biological Report*, 90 (23), Fish and Wildlife Service, US Department of the Interior, Washington, 1992.

Chapter 3 Identification and distribution

Conder P, 'Dusky flying-fox *Pteropus brunneus*', in Strahan R (ed), *Mammals of Australia*, Reed Books, Sydney, 1995: pp 433–34.

Flannery TF, *Mammals of New Guinea*, Robert Brown and Associates, Carina, Qld, 1990.

Hall LS, 'Bare-backed flying-fox *Dobsonia moluccensis*', in Strahan R (ed), *Mammals of Australia*, Reed Books, Sydney, 1995: pp 430–31.

——, 'Black flying-fox *Pteropus alecto*, in Strahan R (ed), *Mammals of Australia*, Reed Books, Sydney, 1995: pp 432–33.

——, 'Identification, distribution and taxonomy of Australian flying-foxes', *Australian Mammalogy*, 10, 1987: pp 75–80.

——, 'Large-eared flying-fox *Pteropus macrotis*', in Strahan R (ed), *Mammals of Australia*, Reed Books, Sydney, 1995: pp 438–39.

Hall LS and Richards GC, *Bats of Eastern Australia*, Booklet No 12, Queensland Museum, Brisbane, 1979.

Hall LS, Richards GC and Spencer HJ, 'Eastern tube-nosed bat *Nyctimene robinsoni*', in Strahan R (ed), *Mammals of Australia*, Reed Books, Sydney, 1995: pp 426–28.

Law BS and Spencer HJ, 'Common blossom bat *Syconycteris australis*', in Strahan R (ed), *Mammals of Australia*, Reed Books, Sydney, 1995: pp 423–25.

McCoy M, 'Little red flying-fox *Pteropus scapulatus*', in Strahan R (ed), *Mammals of Australia*, Reed Books, Sydney, 1995: pp 441–43.

McKean JL, McCoy M and Spencer HJ, 'Northern blossom bat *Macroglossus minimus*', in Strahan R (ed), *Mammals of Australia*, Reed Books, Sydney, 1995: pp 421–22.

Reardon TD and Flavel SC, *Guide to the bats of South Australia*, South Australian Museum, Adelaide, 1987.

Richards GC, 'Torresian flying-fox *Pteropus* sp.', in Strahan R (ed), *Mammals of Australia*, Reed Books, Sydney, 1995: pp 443–44.

——, 'Torresian tube-nosed bat *Nyctimene vizcaccia*', in Strahan R (ed), *Mammals of Australia*, Reed Books, Sydney, 1995: p 429.

Richards GC and Hall LS, 'A new fruit bat of the genus *Pteropus* (Chiroptera: Pteropodidae) from Torres Strait, Australia', *Australian Zoologist*, forthcoming.

Thompson BG, *Field guide to bats of the Northern Territory*, Conservation Commission of the Northern Territory, Darwin, 1991.

Tidemann CR, 'Grey-headed flying-fox *Pteropus poliocephalus*', in Strahan R (ed), *Mammals of Australia*, Reed Books, Sydney, 1995: pp 439–41.

Chapter 4 Anatomy and physiology

Bennett MB, 'Structural modifications involved in the fore- and hind-limb grip of some flying-foxes (Chiroptera: Pteropodidae)', *Journal of Zoology*, 229, 1993: pp 237–48.

Bartholomew GA, Leitner P and Nelson JE, 'Body temperature, oxygen consumption and heart rate in three species of Australian flying-foxes', *Physiological Zoology*, 37, 1964: pp 179–98.

Calford MB and McNally KI, 'Hearing in flying-foxes (Chiroptera: Pteropodidae)', *Australian Mammalogy*, 10, 1987: pp 97–100.

Calford MB, Wise LZ and Pettigrew JD, 'Audiogram of the grey-headed flying-fox, *Pteropus poliocephalus* (Megachiroptera: Pteropodidae)', *Australian Mammalogy*, 8, 1985: pp 309–12.

Calford MB, Graydon ML, Huerta MF, Kaas JH and Pettigrew JD, 'Variant of the mammalian somatopic map in a bat', *Nature*, 313, 1985: pp 477–79.

Carpenter RE, 'Flight physiology of flying foxes, Pteropus poliocephalus', *Journal of Experimental Biology*, 114, 1985: pp 619–47.

Chapman A, Hall LS and Bennett MB, 'Sexual dimorphism in the pelvic girdle of Australian flying-foxes', *Australian Journal of Zoology*, 42, 1994: pp 261–65.

Coburn DK and Geiser F, 'Daily torpor and energy savings in a subtropical blossom bat, *Syconycteris australis* (Megachiroptera)', in Geiser F, Hulbert AJ and Nicol SC (eds), *Adaptations to the cold*, Tenth International Hibernation Symposium, University of New England Press, Armidale, 1996: pp 39–45.

Cool SM, Bennett MB and Romaniuk K, 'Age estimation of pteropodid bats (Megachiroptera) from hard tissue parameters', *Australian Wildlife Research*, 21, 1994: pp 353–64.

Crowley GV and Hall LS, 'Histological observations on the wing of the grey-headed flying-fox (*Pteropus poliocephalus*) (Chiroptera: Pteropodidae)', *Australian Journal of Zoology*, 42, 1994: pp 215–31.

Geiser F, Coburn DK, Kortner G and Law BS, 'Thermoregulation, energy metabolism, and torpor in blossom bats, *Syconycteris australis* (Megachiroptera)', *Journal of Zoology*, London, 239, 1996: pp 583–90.

Graydon M, Giorgi P and Pettigrew J, 'Vision in flying-foxes (Chiroptera: Pteropodidae)', *Australian Mammalogy*, 10, 1987: pp 101–106.

Graydon ML, Pettigrew JD and Giorgi PP, 'Retino-thalamic connections in Megachiroptera', *Neuroscience Letters Supplement*, 23, 1986: pp S50.

Nelson JE, 'Pteropodidae', in Walton DW and Richardson BJ (eds), *Fauna of Australia*, vol. 1b, Australian Government Publishing Service, Canberra, 1989: pp 836–44.

Pettigrew JD, 'Flying primates? Megabats have the advanced pathway from eye to midbrain', *Science*, 231, 1986: pp 1304–1306.

Rosa MGP, Schmid LM, Krubitzer LA and Pettigrew JD, 'Retinotopic organization of the primary visual cortex of flying foxes (*Pteropus poliocephalus* and *Pteropus scapulatus*)', *Journal of Comparative Neurology*, 335, 1993: pp 55–72.

Swartz SM, Bennett MB and Carrier DR, 'Wing bone stresses in free flying bats and the evolution of skeletal design for flight', *Nature* (London), 359, 1992: pp 726–29.

Chapter 5 Reproduction and life cycle

Martin L, Kennedy JH, Little L, Luckhoff H, O'Brien GM, Pow CST, Towers PA, Waldon AK and Wang DY, 'The reproductive biology of Australian flying-foxes (genus *Pteropus*)', *Symposium of the Zoological Society of London*, 67, 1996: pp 167–84.

Martin L, Towers PA, McGuckin MA, Little L, Luckhoff H and Blackshaw A, 'Reproductive biology of flying-foxes (Chiroptera: Pteropodidae)', *Australian Mammalogy*, 10, 1987: pp 115–18.

McGuckin MA and Blackshaw AW, 'Effects of photoperiod on the reproductive physiology of male flying-foxes, *Pteropus poliocephalus*', *Reproduction Fertility and Development*, 4, 1992: pp 43–53.

——, 'Seasonal changes in testicular size, plasma testosterone concentration and body weight in captive flying-foxes (*Pteropus poliocephalus* and *P. scapulatus*)', *Journal of Reproduction and Fertility*, 92, 1991: pp 339–46.

O'Brien GM, 'Seasonal reproduction in flying-foxes, reviewed in the context of other tropical mammals', *Reproduction Fertility and Development*, 5, 1993: pp 499–521.

Pierson ED and Rainey WE, 'The biology of flying-foxes of the genus Pteropus: A review', in Wilson DE and Graham GL (eds), *Pacific Island flying-foxes: Proceedings of an International Conservation Conference*, United States Department of the Interior, Fish and Wildlife Service, Washington.

Pow CST and Martin L, 'The ovarian-uterine vasculature in relation to unilateral endometrial growth in flying-foxes (genus Pteropus, suborder Megachiroptera, order Chiroptera)', *Journal of Reproduction and Fertility*, 101, 1994: pp 247–55.

Webb NJ and Tidemann CR, 'Hybridisation between Black (*Pteropus alecto*) and Grey-headed (*P. poliocephalus*) flying-foxes (Megachiroptera: Pteropodidae)', *Australian Mammalogy*, 18, 1995: pp 19–26.

Vardon MJ and Tidemann CR, 'Reproduction, growth and maturity in the black flying-fox, *Pteropus alecto* (Megachiroptera: Pteropodidae)', *Australian Journal of Zoology*, 46, 1998: pp 329–44.

Chapter 6 Mortality and disease

Allison FR, 'Notes on the bat flies (Diptera: Nycteribiidae) of Australian Megachiroptera', *Australian Mammalogy*, 10, 1987: pp 111–14.

Field HE, McCall BJ and Barrett J, 'Australian Bat Lyssavirus in a captive juvenile Black Flying-fox (*Pteropus alecto*) with implications for in-contact humans', *Emerging Infectious Diseases*, 5, 1998: pp 438–40.

Field HE, Young PL, Johara Mohd Yob, Mills J, Hall LS and Mackenzie JS, 'The natural history of Hendra and Nipah viruses', in Eaton B (ed), Hendra and Nipah viruses, *Microbes and Infection*, forthcoming.

Hall LS, Halpin K and Birt P, 'Fruitful discoveries', *Wildlife Australia*, 34, 1997: pp 8–14.

Pavey CR, 'Food of the Powerful Owl, *Ninox strenua,* in suburban Brisbane, Queensland', *Emu*, 95, 1995: pp 231–32.

Prociv P, 'Observations on the prevalence and possible infection source of *Toxocara pteropodis* (Nematoda: Ascaridoidea)', *Australian Mammalogy*, 8, 1985: pp 319–23.

——, 'Parasites of Australian flying-foxes (Chiroptera: Pteropodidae)', *Australian Mammalogy*, 10, 1987: pp 107–10.

Sutton RH and Hariono B, 'Lead poisoning in Grey-headed fruit bats (*Pteropus poliocephalus*)', *Journal of Wildlife Diseases*, 19, 1983: pp 294–96.

Chapter 7 Behaviour

Birt P and Markus N, 'Notes on the temporary displacement of *Pteropus alecto* and *P. poliocephalus* by *P. scapulatus* within a daytime campsite', *Australian Mammalagy*, 21, 1998: pp 107–10.

Eby P, 'Interactions between the Grey-headed flying-fox *Pteropus poliocephalus* (Chiroptera: Pteropodidae) and its diet plants: seasonal movements and seed dispersal', PhD thesis, University of New England, Armidale, 1997.

Hall LS and Richards GC, 'Flying-fox camps', *Wildlife Australia*, 28, 1991: pp 19–22.

Law B, 'The lunar cycle influences time of roost departure in the Common blossom bat, *Syconycteris australis*', *Australian Mammalogy*, 20, 1997: pp 21–24.

Nelson JE, 'Behaviour of Australian Pteropodidae (Megachiroptera)', *Animal Behaviour*, 13, 1965: pp 544–57.

——, 'Vocal communication in Australian flying-foxes (Pteropodidae: Megachiroptera)', *Zeitschrift fur Tierpsychologie*, 21, 1964: pp 857–70.

Prociv P, 'Seasonal behaviour of *Pteropus scapulatus* (Chiroptera : Pteropodidae)', *Australian Mammalogy*, 6, 1983: pp 45–46.

Puddicombe R, 'A behavioural study of the Grey-headed Flying-fox *Pteropus poliocephalus* (Megachiroptera)', BSc. Hons thesis, University of New England, Armidale, 1981.

Richards GC, 'The Spectacled flying-fox, *Pteropus conspicillatus*, in North Queensland: 1. Roost site selection and distribution patterns', *Australian Mammalogy*, 13, 1990: pp 17–24.

Spencer H and Fleming T, 'Preliminary observations on the roosting and foraging behaviour of the Queensland tube-nosed bat, *Nyctimene robinsoni*, (Pteropodidae) obtained by radiotracking', *Australian Wildlife Research*, 16, 1989: pp 413–20.

Stager KE and Hall LS, 'A cave roosting colony of the Black flying-fox (*Pteropus alecto*) in Queensland, Australia', *Journal of Mammalogy*, 64, 1983: pp 223–25.

Ratcliffe FN, 'Notes on the fruit bats (*Pteropus* spp.) of Australia', *Journal of Animal Ecology*, 1, 1932: pp 32–57.

Tidemann CR, Vardon MJ, Loughland RA and Brocklehurst PA, 'Dry season camps of flying-foxes (*Pteropus* spp.) in Kakadu World Heritage Area, north Australia', *Journal of Zoology* (London), 247, 1999: pp 155–63.

Chapter 8 Diet and feeding ecology

Birt P, Hall LS and Smith GC, 'Ecomorphology of Australian megachiropteran (Chiroptera: Pteropodidae) tongues', *Australian Journal of Zoology*, 45, 1997: pp 369–84.

Clemson A, *Honey and pollen flora*, Inkata Press, Melbourne, 1985.

Eby P, '"Finger-winged night workers": managing forests to conserve the role of Grey-headed Flying-foxes as pollinators and seed dispersers', in Lunney D (ed), *Conservation of Australia's forest fauna*, Royal Zoological Society of New South Wales, Mosman, 1991: pp 91–100.

Eby P, 'An analysis of diet specialization in frugivorous *Pteropus poliocephalus* (Megachiroptera) in Australian subtropical rainforests', *Australian Journal of Ecology*, 23, 1998: pp 443–56.

——, 'Seasonal movements of Grey-headed Flying-foxes *Pteropus poliocephalus* (Chiroptera: Pteropodidae), from two maternity camps in northern New South Wales', *Australian Wildlife Research*, 18, 1991: pp 547–59.

Faegri K and van der Pijl L, *The principles of pollination ecology*, Pergamon Press, New York, 1971.

Fujita MS, *Flying-fox (Chiroptera: Pteropodidae) pollination, seed dispersal, and economic importance*, Resource publication no. 2b, Conservation International, Austin, USA, 1991.

Hall LS and Pettigrew JD, 'The bat with the stereo nose', *Australian Natural History*, 24, 1995: pp 26–28.

Law BS, 'Maintenance nitrogen requirements of the Queensland blossom bat (*Syconycteris australis*) on a sugar/pollen diet: is nitrogen a limiting resource?', *Physiological Zoology*, 65, 3, 1992: pp 634–48.

Lowry FB, 'Green-leaf fractionation by fruit bats: is this feeding behaviour a unique nutritional strategy for herbivores?', *Australian Wildlife Research*, 16, 1989: pp 203–206.

Marshall AG, 'Old World phytophagous bats (Megachiroptera) and their food plants: a survey', *Zoological Journal of the Linnean Society*, 83, 1985: pp 351–69.

McCoy M, 'Pollination of eucalypts by flying-foxes in northern Australia', in Slack JM (ed), *Flying-fox Workshop Proceedings*, New South Wales Department of Agriculture and Fisheries, Sydney, 1990: pp 33–37.

McWilliam AN, 'The feeding ecology of *Pteropus* in north-eastern New South Wales, Australia', *Myotis*, 23–24, 1986: pp 201–208.

Parry-Jones K and Augee ML, 'Food selection by Grey-headed Flying-foxes (*Pteropus poliocephalus*) occupying a summer colony site near Gosford, New South Wales', *Australian Wildlife Research*, 18, 1991: pp 111–24.

Richards GC, 'Aspects of the ecology of Spectacled Flying-foxes, *Pteropus conspicillatus* (Chiroptera: Pteropodidae) in North Queensland', *Australian Mammalogy*, 10, 1987: pp 87–88.

——, 'The Spectacled flying-fox, *Pteropus conspicillatus*, in North Queensland: Part 2, Diet, feeding ecology and seed dispersal', *Australian Mammalogy*, 13, 1990: pp 25–31.

Richards GC and Prociv P, 'Folivory in *Pteropus*', *Australian Bat Research News*, 20, 1984: pp 13–14.

Start AN and Marshall AG, 'Nectarivorous bats as pollinators in west Malaysia', in Barley J and Styles BT (eds), *Variation, breeding and conservation of tropical forest trees*, Academic Press, London, 1976: pp 141–50.

Stellar DC, 'The dietary energy and nitrogen requirements of the Grey-headed Flying-fox, *Pteropus poliocephalus* (Temminck) (Megachiroptera)', *Australian Journal of Zoology*, 34, 1986: pp 339–49.

Tedman RA and Hall LS, 'The absorptive surface of the small intestine of *Pteropus poliocephalus* (Megachiroptera: Pteropodidae): an important factor in rapid food transit?', *Australian Mammalogy*, 8, 1985: pp 271–78.

——, 'The morphology of the gastrointestinal tract and food transit time in the fruit bats *Pteropus alecto* and *P.poliocephalus* (Megachiroptera)', *Australian Journal of Zoology*, 33, 1985: pp 625–40.

van der Pijl L, 'The dispersal of plants by bats (Chiropterochory)', *Acta Botanica Neerlandica*, 6, 1957: pp 291–395.

Chapter 9 Migration

Eby P, 'Seasonal movements of Grey-headed flying-foxes, *Pteropus poliocephalus* (Chiroptera: Pteropodidae), from two maternity camps in northern New South Wales', *Australian Wildlife Research*, 18, 1991: pp 547–59.

Hall LS, 'Predicting flying fox movements in southeast Queensland: when, why and where', in *Bird and Bat Control Seminar Proceedings*, Nambour, 1994: pp 30–37, Queensland Department of Primary Industries, Brisbane.

Law BS, '*Banksia* nectar and pollen: Dietary items affecting the abundance of the common blossom bat, *Syconycteris australis* in southeastern Australia', *Australian Journal of Ecology*, 19, 4, 1994: pp 425–34.

——, 'The effect of energy supplementation on the local abundance of the common blossom bat *Syconycteris australis* in southeast Australia', *Oikos*, 72, 1, 1995: pp 42–50.

——, 'Physiological factors affecting pollen use by the Queensland Blossom Bat (*Syconycteris australis*)', *Functional Ecology*, 6, 1992: pp 257–64.

——, 'Roosting and foraging ecology of the Queensland blossom bat (*Syconycteris australis*) in north-eastern New South Wales: flexibility in response to seasonal variation', *Australian Wildlife Research*, 20, 1993: pp 419–31.

Lunney D and Moon C, 'Flying-foxes and their camps in the remnant rainforests of north-east New South Wales', in Dargavel J (ed), *Australia's ever-changing forests*, part 3, Proceedings of the Third National Conference on Australian Forest History, CRES, Canberra, 1997: pp 247–77.

Nelson JE, 'Movements of Australian flying-foxes (Pteropodidae: Megachiroptera)', *Australian Journal of Zoology*, 13, 1965: pp 53–73.

Palmer C and Woinarski JCZ, 'Seasonal roosts and foraging movements of the black flying fox (*Pteropus alecto*) in the Northern Territory: resource tracking in a landscape mozaic', *Wildlife Research*, 26, 1999: pp 823–38.

Parry-Jones K, '*Pteropus poliocephalus* (Chiroptera: Pteropodidae) in New South Wales', *Australian Mammalogy*, 10, 1987: pp 81–85.

Parry-Jones K and Augee ML, 'Movements of Grey-headed flying-foxes (*Pteropus poliocephalus*) to and from a colony site on the central coast of New South Wales', *Australian Wildlife Research*, 19, 1992: pp 331–40.

Ratcliffe FN, 'The flying-fox (*Pteropus*) in Australia', *Bulletin of the Council for Scientific and Industrial Research, Australia*, 53, 1931: pp 1–80.

Spencer HJ and Fleming TH, 'Roosting and foraging behaviour of the Queensland tube-nosed bat, *Nyctimene robinsoni*, Pteropodidae: preliminary radio-tracking observations', *Australian Wildlife Research*, 16, 1989: pp 413–20.

Webb NJ and Tidemann CR, 'Mobility of Australian flying-foxes, *Pteropus* spp. (Megachiroptera): Evidence from genetic variation', *Proceedings of the Royal Society*, (London) series B, 263, 1996: pp 497–502.

Chapter 10 Conservation and management

Birt P, Markus N, Collins L and Hall L, 'Urban flying-foxes', *Nature Australia*, 26, 1998: pp 54–59.

Eby P, *The biology and management of flying-foxes in NSW: Species management*, report no.18, New South Wales National Parks and Wildlife Service, Sydney, 1995.

——, 'The ecology of grey-headed flying foxes and implications for their management' in *Bird and Bat Seminar Proceedings*, Nambour, 1994: pp 23–29. Queensland Department of Primary Industries, Brisbane.

Eby P, 'Finger-winged night workers: managing forests to conserve the role of Grey-headed Flying Foxes as pollinators and seed dispersers', in Lunney D (ed) *Conservation of Australia's forest fauna*, Royal Zoological Society of New South Wales, Sydney, 1991: pp 91–100.

Eby P, Richards G, Collins L and Parry-Jones K, 'The distribution, abundance and vulnerability to population reduction of a nomadic nectarivore, the Grey-headed flying fox, *Pteropus poliocephalus* in New South Wales, during a period of resource concentration', *Australian Zoologist*, 31, 1999: pp 240–53.

Fleming PJS and Robinson D, 'Flying-fox (Chiroptera: Pteropodidae) on the north coast of New South Wales: Damage to stonefruit crops and control methods', *Australian Mammalogy*, 10, 1987: pp 143–45.

Hall LS, 'Bat conservation in Australia', *Australian Zoologist*, 26, 1990: pp 1–4.

Hall LS and Richards GC, 'Crop protection and management of flying-foxes (Chiroptera : Pteropodidae)', *Australian Mammalogy*, 10, 1987: pp 137–39.

——, 'The flying-fox problem in eastern Australia', in *Proceedings of the 1987 Australian Vertebrate Pest Control Conference*, Coolangatta, 1987: pp 279–83.

Richards GC, 'The conservation of forest bats in Australia: Do we really know the problems and solutions?', in Lunney D (ed), *Conservation of Australia's forest fauna*, Royal Zoological Society of New South Wales, Sydney, 1991: pp 81–90.

——, 'The conservation status of the rainforest bat fauna of North Queensland', in Werren GL and Kershaw AP (eds), *The rainforest legacy: Australian national rainforests study*, vol. 2, *Flora and fauna of the rainforests*, Special Australian Heritage Publications, series no. 7 (2), Australian Government Printing Service, Canberra, 1992: pp 177–86.

——, 'Rainforest bat conservation: Unique problems in a unique environment', *Australian Zoologist*, 26, 1990: pp 44–46.

Richards GC, Eby P and Parry-Jones K 'Estimating the Grey-headed Flying-fox population: an example of community involvement in bat conservation', *Australasian Bat Society Newsletter*, 11, 1995: pp 26–28.

Richards GC and Hall LS, 'The conservation biology of Australian bats: are recent advances solving our problems?', in Kunz TH and Racey PA (eds), *Bat biology and conservation*, Smithsonian Institution Press, Washington, 1998: pp 271–81.

Sinclair EA, Webb NJ, Marchant AD and Tidemann CR, 'Genetic variation in the little red flying-fox *Pteropus scapulatus* (Megachiroptera: Pteropodidae): implications for management', *Biological Conservation*, 76, 1996: pp 45–50.

Tidemann CR and Vardon MJ, 'Pests, pestilence, pollen and pot-roasts: the need for community-based management of flying-foxes in Australia', *Australian Biologist*, 10, 1997: pp 79–85.

Tidemann CR, Vardon MJ, Nelson JE, Speare R and Gleeson L, 'Health and conservation implications of Australian bat *Lyssavirus*', *Australian Zoologist*, 1997: pp 369–76.

Vardon MJ, Simpson BK, Sherwell D and Tidemann CR, 'Flying foxes and tourists: a conservation dilemma in the Northern Territory', *Australian Zoologist*, 30, 3, 1997: pp 310–15.

Wahl DE, 'The management of flying-foxes (*Pteropus* spp.) in New South Wales', Masters thesis, University of Canberra, Canberra, 1994.

Chapter 11 Rehabilitation and rearing

Collins L, *Hand-rearing and development of the orphan flying-fox*, FICN, Nimbin, New South Wales, 1995.

George H, 'Grey-headed flying foxes' in Hand SJ (ed), *Care and handling of Australian native animals*, Surrey Beatty and Sons, Sydney, 1990: pp 159–69.

Luckhoff H, 'Rearing orphan *Pteropus* spp (Chiroptera: Pteropodidae) for release in the wild', *Australian Mammalogy*, 10, 1987: pp 127–28.

Markus N and Blackshaw J, 'Motivations and characteristics of volunteer flying-fox rehabilitators in Australia', *Anthrozoos*, 11, 4, 1998: pp 203–209.

Markus N and Valzacchi N, *Orphan flying-fox hand-raising procedures*, Currumbin Sanctuary, Currumbin (Queensland), 1996.

Martin L, 'Posture and anatomical adaptations in neonatal flying-foxes (Genus Pteropus, suborder Megachiroptera): cautionary tales for carers', *Australian Zoologist*, 30, 4, 1998: pp 443–48.

Minogue T and Luckhoff H, *Gentle method for raising orphan flying-foxes*, Orphan Native Animal Rear and Release Programme, Darra (Queensland), 1995.

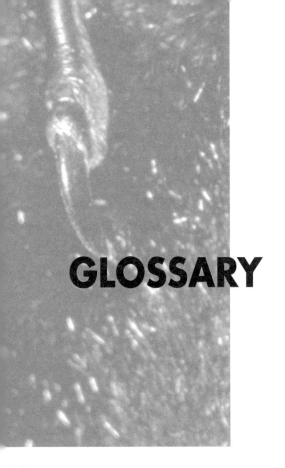

GLOSSARY

WORDS IN *ITALICS* ARE LISTED ELSEWHERE IN THE GLOSSARY.

acrosome	the membrane covering the head of sperm, responsible for the penetration of the egg for fertilisation
aerodynamic	the shape of parts of an animal to make flight as easy as possible and at the lowest energy cost
alkaloids	chemicals including those, usually toxic or distasteful, found in native fruits and leaves that the plant produces for protection from frugivores and herbivores
angiosperm	flowering plants; literal meaning is that the seeds are protected by an ovary (see *gymnosperm*)
anthers	the portion of the *stamen* that contains the pollen
antibodies	proteins produced in response to a virus to counteract its effect
apical	at or towards the apex (tip) of something
asynchronous	at different times (eg fruiting in different times or seasons)
audiograms	measurements of what frequencies an animal can hear
baculum	a bone located in the tip of the penis in male Megachiroptera
caecum	a pouch at the junction of the small and large intestines
camps	the colloquial term that describes roosting sites of flying foxes
caudal	at or towards the tail-end of the body

cauliflorous	flowering and fruiting from the trunk of a tree (or on branches)
cerebellum	the part of the brain at the back of the skull that co-ordinates muscles, posture, balance and movements
cerebral cortex	the major part of the brain located at the front of the skull that interprets sensory information, and co-ordinates sensory and neural functions including memory, pattern recognition, and vocalisation
cervical	related to the neck·
chiropterophilous (plants)	plants which rely on bats, usually in the context of pollination and seed dispersal
chitin	a compound found in insects, particularly the exoskeleton
choroid	one of the inner layers lining the eye
circumvallate	large round *papilla* on the tongue surface, surrounded by a channel which contains taste buds
clavicle	the collar bone
cochlea	area in the inner ear where sound waves are translated to nervous signals
corolla	the whorls of petals forming a flower
dactylopatagium	the wing membrane between the forelimb digits
dental formula	the count of the number of teeth, written as: incisors + canines + premolars + molars = total number
dietary guild	a group of several (or many) different species of animals that all feed on the same type of food
dorsal	of or towards the back
echolocation	the interpretation of the echoes of sounds made by an animal, by which it 'sees' its surroundings
El Niño	the irregular warming of the South Pacific Ocean surface which influences weather patterns in Australia
encephalitis	inflammation or infection of the brain
endemic	found only in one country
endometrium	the lining of the uterus
Eocene	a geological period spanning 58-35 million years ago
epidermis	surface skin
epididymis	a duct behind the testes of mammals in which sperm travels to the vas deferens
extralimital	related to the distribution of a plant or animal, indicating that it is found in other countries; the opposite of *endemic*
femur	the thick bone between the pelvis and the knee (the thigh bone in humans)
folivorous	eating foliage (leaves etc)
frugivorous	eating fruit
gastrointestinal tract	the entire arrangement of organs from the oesophagus to the anus
gymnosperms	plants such as conifers and cycads that do not have obvious flowers; literally where the seeds are unprotected by an ovary (cf *angiosperm*)
homeotherms	animals that regulate their own body temperature

hydranencephaly	fluid on the brain
hydrocephaly	fluid on the brain
implantation	the attachment of fertilised eggs to the wall of the uterus
inferior colliculus	the auditory area of the brain
inflorescence	a flower-head of a plant that contains the stems, stalks and flowers (eg Banksia)
intine layer (of pollen)	the inner layer that swells and ruptures through the exine (outer) layer during fertilisation
lateral	of or towards the sides
limbic structures	parts of the brain that are thought to focus on emotional states and related behaviour
lumbar	related to the lower back or loin area
mechanoreceptors	a sensory receptor that responds to a physical stimulus such as touch or sound
medial	of or towards the middle
morphological	related to the shape of parts of the body
muscle myopathy	degeneration or wastage of muscle tissue
nectarivorous/ nectariferous	feeding on nectar (and usually pollen) of plants
neocortex	the highest centres of integration in the cortex of the brain
occipitopollicalis	muscle from the arm to the thumb that forms the leading edge muscle of the wing; forms the forward edge of the *propatagium*
olfactory bulb	the primary brain centre that senses smell
outbreeding	fertilising from the pollen of another plant of the same species (see *self-pollination*)
outcrossing	a type of pollination where fertilisation is carried out by transferring pollen from one plant to another (see *self-pollination*)
palate	the roof of the mouth
papillae	protuberances or small fleshy projections in parts of organs of the body
patella	kneecap
pathogens	an agent such as a virus or bacteria that causes disease
pectoralis muscle	a muscle in the chest, used in the downstroke of the wing
phenology	the flowering and fruiting patterns of plants
pheromones	chemical substances or aromas secreted and released by an animal for territorial marking or other passive communication
photosensitive	something that reacts chemically or electrically to light
phytophagous	feed on plant products
plagiopatagium	the wing membrane that extends from the body and hind limb to the arm and fifth digit
Pleistocene	a geological period that commenced around 2 million years ago
pollen vector	an organism or physical action that transports pollen from one flower to another
population viability	the ability of a group of animals to maintain their population numbers, where births and deaths are either equal or births are greater than deaths, and reproduction can successfully occur

porancephaly	a brain disease
procumbent	prostrate; in the description of bat teeth it indicates facing forward (as in 'buck-teeth')
propagules	the result of plant reproduction (usually seeds, but often the whole fruit is referred to as a propagule)
propatagium	the wing membrane that extends from the arm to the leading edge and the thumb
quadrupedal	having four limbs
radius	the main bone of the forearm
retina	the light sensitive coat of the inner eye
retinotectal fibres	nerve fibres which carry information from the eye (retina) to the brain
retinothalmic fibres	nerve fibres which carry information from the eye (retina) to the brain
riparian	along rivers
rostral	of or toward the nose or snout
saccular	sack or bag shaped
sagittal crest	a raised section of bone on top of the skull to which the jaw muscles are attached
scapula	the shoulder blade
self-pollination	where fertilisation is carried out by transferring pollen within the one plant (see *outcrossing*)
seminal vesicles	the tubes that convey semen
seminiferous cycle	the cycle of production of semen
somatosensory map	a diagram of how the brain senses the body
stamen	the male fertilising organ of a flower that holds the *anther* and its pollen
sternum	the breast bone, or keel
superior colliculus	part of the brain where vision is interpreted
sympatric	found at the same locality
synchronous	occurring at the same time
thermoregulation	the physiological process of keeping the body at an optimal temperature when air temperatures are warmer or cooler than body temperature
torpor	the lowering of body temperature and metabolism from normal to conserve energy
ultrasonic	above the highest frequency of human hearing, usually over 20 kHz
uropatagium	the membrane that connects between the tail and the hind legs
vascular	of the vessels that carry blood or sap
vector	a carrier of something else, such as disease or pollen
ventral	of or toward the abdomen or abdominal surface (front)
villi	finger-like protrusions on a surface
visual acuity	the precision or sharpness of sight
visual cortex	the part of the brain that co-ordinates sight

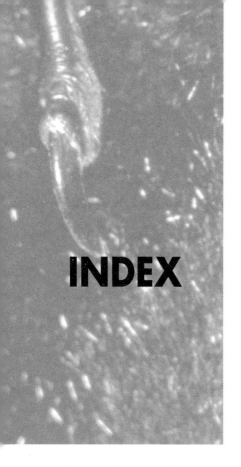

INDEX

Page numbers in *italics* refer to illustrations, and plates refer to the colour photographs found in a separate section in the book.